Introducing Discourse An

Introducing Discourse Analysis: From Grammar to Society is a concise and accessible introduction by bestselling author, James Paul Gee, to the fundamental ideas behind different specific approaches to discourse analysis, or the analysis of language in use. The book stresses how grammar sets up choices for speakers and writers to make, choices which express, not unvarnished truth, but perspectives or viewpoints on reality. In turn, these perspectives are the material from which social interactions, social relations, identity, and politics make and remake society and culture. The book also offers an approach to how discourse analysis can contribute to lessening the ideological divides and echo chambers that so bedevil our world today. Organized in a user-friendly way with short numbered sections and recommended readings, *Introducing Discourse Analysis* is an essential primer for all students of discourse analysis within linguistics, education, communication studies, and related areas.

James Paul Gee is Mary Lou Fulton Presidential Professor of Literacy Studies and Regents' Professor at Arizona State University, USA. He is author of a number of books, including *How to do Discourse Analysis, Second Edition* (Routledge, 2014), *An Introduction to Discourse Analysis, Fourth Edition* (Routledge, 2014), and *Language and Learning in the Digital Age* (Routledge, 2011). He is also the co-editor of *The Routledge Handbook of Discourse Analysis* (2011).

Introducing Discourse Analysis

From Grammar to Society

James Paul Gee

Routledge
Taylor & Francis Group

LONDON AND NEW YORK

First published 2018
by Routledge
2 Park Square, Milton Park, Abingdon, Oxon OX14 4RN

and by Routledge
711 Third Avenue, New York, NY 10017

Routledge is an imprint of the Taylor & Francis Group, an informa business

British Library Cataloguing-in-Publication Data
A catalogue record for this book is available from the British Library

Library of Congress Cataloging-in-Publication Data
Names: Gee, James Paul, author.
Title: Introducing Discourse Analysis : from grammar to society / James
Paul Gee.
Description: New York, NY : Routledge, 2018. | Includes bibliographical
references and index.
Identifiers: LCCN 2017023854| ISBN 9781138298347 (hardback) |
ISBN 9781138298385 (pbk.) | ISBN 9781351580878 (epub) | ISBN
9781351580861 (mobipocket/kindle)
Subjects: LCSH: Discourse analysis.
Classification: LCC P302 .G3976 2018 | DDC 401/.41–dc23
LC record available at https://lccn.loc.gov/2017023854

ISBN: 978-1-138-29834-7 (hbk)
ISBN: 978-1-138-29838-5 (pbk)
ISBN: 978-1-315-09869-2 (ebk)

Typeset in Bembo
by Sunrise Setting Ltd, Brixham, UK

Visit the companion website: http://routledgetextbooks.com/
textbooks/_author/gee-9780415725569/

Contents

Preface

Discourse analysis is the study of what we humans do with language and how we do it. We don't use language just to give each other information. We humans also use language to think, plan, and dream; to fashion and refashion our identities; to bond with, or show deference towards others; to express emotions; to collaborate or manipulate; to carry out actions, projects, and activism of all different sorts; to form and maintain (or break apart) social relationships; and to change the world in ways big and small.

Discourse analysis is a big field made up of many different relatively small groups, each doing discourse analysis in their own way; each using their own terminology and defending their own theories of language, communication, and society. It can be hard to know if these different approaches disagree or just use words differently. Even when it is clear they disagree, it is hard to know how to adjudicate the disagreement across terminological, disciplinary, and theoretical differences.

But all is not chaos. Underneath all the diversity, there are some "big ideas" that many different approaches have allegiance to, though they express that allegiance in different ways. This book is meant to discuss the forest and not get lost among the trees. It is meant to offer a viewpoint on the big ideas that make discourse analysis interesting and important, ideas that then take shape in different ways in different approaches.

The book is meant for serious beginners; it is meant for my fellow discourse researchers who want to develop their own view of what can unite us or, at least, allow us to have wider discussions; and for academics working in other areas who want to use discourse analysis in tandem with other methods. My goal is not for readers to follow me, but just to join in a discussion about what can unite us and lead to more inclusive discussions.

This book does, however, draw one line in the sand. Some approaches to discourse analysis ignore grammar. These approaches tend to focus on themes in talk and text, but do not offer evidence for their analyses based on the structural and functional properties of language. I do not develop any specific theory of grammar in this book. Here, again, I stick to the big picture. But I do stress that grammar is the instrument that allows us to play the tunes that make meaning in the world.

Discourse—language-in-use—goes well beyond grammar, but its origins, nonetheless, are in grammar as the set of choices our language allows us to make about how to say what we say. So, this book tries to be clear about the connections between grammar and discourse and even grammar and society, while still showing that discourse analysis goes places grammar cannot go.

This book draws on some ideas and data from my earlier books (*An Introduction to Discourse Analysis: Theory and Method*, Fourth Edition, 2014, and *How to Do Discourse Analysis: A Toolkit*, Second Edition, 2014, both from Routledge), but seeks to stake out new and higher ground. In this book, I do not discuss discourse analysis of multimodal "texts", ones which meld images and words, for example. However, for those interested in my views here, see: *Unified Discourse Analysis: Language, Reality, Virtual Worlds, and Video Games*, also from Routledge (2014). As this paragraph shows, Routledge (and, in particular, my editor, motivator, sustainer, and guide at the press, Louisa Semlyen) has been the conduit of my work on discourse analysis. For this I am deeply grateful.

1

Preliminaries on language

1.1 The word "language"

This chapter deals with very basic preliminaries. Many readers may well be familiar with these ideas. Nonetheless, it is important for us to agree on "the basics" at the beginning of our journey, or, at least, for you to know what I take the basics to be. So, first, we turn to what the word "language" will mean in this book.

The word "language" has a lot of different meanings. Consider just some of them below:

1. The English language
2. The language of the Bible
3. A computer language
4. Secret languages
5. Child language
6. The language of street gangs
7. The language of bees
8. The language of life (DNA)
9. The language of love
10. Legal language

To do discourse analysis, we need to be more specific about what we will mean by "language". I will mean by the word "language" what linguists call "natural languages". These are the languages that humans acquire as their first or "native" language (some people have more than one native language). Such languages are unique to us as a species. While many types of animals have communication systems, only humans have language as we humans know it (Safina 2015). Natural languages have two properties that no animal communication system has (Pinker 1994):

A. Recursive syntax

Human languages are made up of units that can fit into larger units that themselves can fit into yet larger units, and so on indefinitely. It's like boxes inside boxes inside boxes forever. There is no upper bound on how big a unit can get:

1a. hat
(a noun)
1b. the hat
(a noun inside a noun phrase)
1c. the hat on my head
(a bigger noun phrase with the prepositional phrase "on my head" inside it)
1d. the quite strikingly red hat on my head
(a yet bigger noun phrase with an adjective phrase "quite strikingly red" and a prepositional phrase "on my head" inside it)
1e. The quite strikingly red hat on my head that I got at a fancy store last week on a shopping trip to New York with my wife
(a yet bigger noun phrase with lots of stuff inside it)

2a. John believes Mary
(a sentence)
2b. Herman thinks [that John believes Mary]
(a sentence "John believes Mary" inside a bigger sentence "Herman thinks that John believes Mary")
2c. Joan hopes [that Herman thinks] [that John believes Mary]
(a sentence inside a bigger sentence inside a yet bigger sentence)
2d. We all know [that Joan hopes] [that Herman thinks] [that John believes Mary]
(a sentence inside a bigger sentence inside a yet bigger sentence inside a yet bigger sentence)

B. Efficacy

There is no limit to the topics any natural language can talk about. Human language is an all-purpose communication device that is not restricted (like animal communication systems) to certain topics or environmental conditions.

These two properties of human language are the grammatical basis for discourse analysis. Grammar includes word choice and choices of how to phrase things (Coulmas & Watts 2006). Grammar offers speakers an infinite number of different ways to say an infinite number of things. Of course, we do not actually use this infinity in our lives. Our lives are too short. But the point of grammar is to offer us different choices about how to say or think what we want to say or think.

For example, consider the sorts of choices below:

1a. Mistakes were made
1b. The company's president made a mistake
1c. To err is human
1d. Unforeseen circumstances intervened
1e. Mistakes happen
1f. It was a real blunder by the boss

2a. Hornworms sure vary a lot in how well they grow
2b. Hornworm growth exhibits a significant amount of variation
2c. Hornworms come in lots of different sizes
2d. *Manduca sexta larva* grow up to 70 millimeters in length, but can vary significantly.

3a. Could you please help me?
3b. I need help
3c. I hate to ask, but could you possibly help me
3d. Get a move on and help me

4a. They are freedom fighters
    (said of people who use terror to attack our enemies)
4b. They are terrorists
    (said of people who use terror to attack us or our allies)
4c. They are guerillas engaged in guerilla warfare
4d. They are Mujahideen engaged in jihad

Imagine that in the case of the utterances in (1) a company spokesperson has been asked why something bad has happened. The spokesperson must choose among all the alternative choices the grammar of his or her language makes available. The available choices are determined by **grammar** (a few of which are listed in 1). The actual choice made is language-in-action—**discourse**—determined by a human being in real time. Saying "mistakes were made" allows the spokesperson to leave out the person or people responsible for the mistakes. Saying (1f) might be a good way for the spokesperson to get fired.

Choices have meaning not just by themselves, but also in relation to all the other choices that were available, but excluded, once a choice was made. If all neckties were black, wearing a black tie would just mean you chose to wear a tie. If there are many colors of ties, then wearing a black one means you did not choose to wear other colors (e.g., brighter ones) for the occasion. And we can then ask why you didn't. So, too, with language.

Choices can allow us to try to capture the truth as we see it; to lie effectively; or to shape how people think without directly lying to them. They allow us to express what we want to say in ways that can reach people's emotions and minds, and even encourage them to act.

We see here an important principle at work, the **principle of choice**. This principle is at the heart of discourse analysis. This principle says that what something means depends both on what we said and on the possible choices we had to pick from in saying it. Both what we picked (the choice we made) and what we didn't (what we excluded) are meaningful and play a role in interpretation. The choices we did not make matter because listeners and readers must ask why we did not make these choices, but another one (why did a person wear a blue tie and not a red one?). Sometimes we make our choices consciously and reflectively and sometimes they are made quickly and unconsciously in the rapid give and take of conversation.

A note on references

There are recommended readings at the end of most numbered sections in this book. These are the sources readers can follow up with to give them a well-rounded background for discourse analysis. There are references at the end of each chapter. These are the sources in which readers can check my claims and see alternate perspectives on my claims. By and large, I cite as references work that I would also recommend people read.

Recommended reading

Edward Sapir (1921). *Language: An Introduction to Speech*. New York: Harcourt Brace. Republished, Mineola, NY: Dover, 2004 (available free on Amazon.com as an e-book).

1.2 Language change

The names we give languages—like English, Russian, Mandarin, and Navajo—are "political". Dutch and German are close enough to each other that they could easily be viewed as dialects of one language. We use different names for them because their speakers live in different countries (one of which invaded the other in World War II) and came to feel not closely aligned with each other. American English and British English differ and they are spoken in different countries. Nonetheless, we use the same name for them because the two countries see themselves as closely aligned and related, despite past hostilities.

Ultimately all human languages in the world come from a one (or, perhaps, a very few) languages that arose in Africa. As people drifted away from each other, this common language changed over time into different versions or "dialects". After a long enough time, these dialects became so different that they constituted different and mutually uninterpretable languages. Yet, as we have just seen, even before dialects have diverged a great deal, they may end up being called different languages because of cultural, historical, or political reasons.

Languages are always changing. If we look across a large expanse of time we can see how much any given language has changed. As an example, consider the Old English below from 1000 CE talking about Noah and the Ark:

Him	þa	Noe	gewat,	swa	hine	nergend	het,
Him	then	Noah	went	as	him	the savior	commanded
under		earce		bord			
on		the ark		board			

Then Noah went on board the Ark as the savior had commanded him.

(https://lrc.la.utexas.edu/eieol/engol/70)

Clearly, Old English sounded quite different than current English and it ordered words in phrases and sentences differently. We can see similarities, but the two languages (or dialects) are not mutually interpretable.

Changes in language happen because different speakers—often unconsciously—innovate in different ways. Languages change, as well, because as children learn them, they sometimes change them. Not all changes catch on, but some do and spread to other speakers. Why some changes spread and others do not is still largely a mystery to linguists.

Here are some examples of changes that spread in English. At one time the word "knight" was pronounced with an initial "k" sound (still retained in the spelling), but it is no longer. The word "bead" used to mean "prayer", but now means a little round ball, because monks used rosaries (strings of little round balls) to say their prayers. The word "orange" used to be pronounced as "norange". Speakers changed "a norange" into "an orange" (and also "a napple" into "an apple"). Children heard "a norange" as "an orange" and the change caught on. As we saw in the Old English example, word order has changed in English as well.

There is a deeper reason for language change, beyond accidents of chance and circumstance. At both a social and a neurological level, children require a native language that is both fast and clear (Slobin 1977). These two goals are in tension with each other. If children inherit a native language that is quite clear, but too slow, they speed things up (e.g., by shortening words, melding things together, or leaving out things altogether). If children inherit a native language that is fast, but not clear enough, they add things back in to create greater clarity.

So, across time, languages swing between the poles of clarity and speed and continually adjust if things go too far in one direction or the other. For example, many languages have case endings on their nouns. Old English, for instance, used the word "docga" to mean dog in subject position ("the dog chased the cat"), but "docgan" to mean dog in direct object position ("the cat chased the dog"). Case endings, if they become too numerous or complex, can slow things down and, thus, they sometimes are dropped by subsequent generations, as they were in later varieties of English (but note our pronouns: *He/she* does not like John; John does not like *him/her*).

However, if case endings on nouns disappear, something else—such as word order (as in modern English)—must be used to distinguish subjects from direct objects (and other noun roles), otherwise there would be a serious threat to clarity. It is word order that tells us that "The dog chased the cat" can only mean the dog is the chaser and not the chased. In some languages with case endings, word order is much freer.

The **principle of fast-and-clear** plays a role in discourse, as well as in grammar. Speakers of all languages use faster, less clear (less explicit) forms of language in some contexts and slower, clearer (more explicit) forms in others. For example, (1a) below is faster, but less clear than is (1b), which is slower but clearer:

1a. What an ass that guy was, you know, her boyfriend. I should hope, if I ever did that to see you, you would shoot the guy.

1b. Well, when I thought about it, I don't know, it seemed to me that Gregory should be the most offensive. He showed no understanding for Abigail, when she told him what she was forced to do. He was callous. He was hypocritical, in the sense that he professed to love her, then acted like that.

(1a) and (1b) were said by the same young woman about the same thing to two different audiences (1a was to her boyfriend and 1b to her parents at dinner). We tend to use faster, but less clear, language when we are communicating with people with whom we share a great deal of knowledge or when we want to let them participate in the interaction more by leaving things for them to imagine or infer for themselves. We tend to use slower, but clearer, language with people with whom we share less background knowledge or with whom we want to be more deferential.

Recommended reading

Jean Berko Gleason and Nan Bernstein Ratner, Eds. (2016). *The Development of Language*. Ninth Edition. Boston, MA: Pearson.
John McWhorter (2016). *Words on the Move: Why English Won't—And Can't—Sit Still (Like Literally)*. New York: Henry Holt.

1.3 Language and isolation

As we said earlier, originally there was probably only one human language that arose in Africa. As people moved out of Africa, different groups became separated from each other. As always, for each group changes happened in how people spoke. But since the groups were now isolated from each other, the changes that spread would have been different for different groups. Over time, each group began to speak a different version ("dialect") of the original language. With more time, the changes became numerous and different enough that eventually the different groups spoke languages that were not mutually interpretable. So, the different groups then could not have understood each other, even if they came back into contact again (Aitchison 2001).

Linguists classify different languages into families based on how they are related historically. For example, Spanish, Italian, French, Portuguese, and Romanian (and other languages) are all in the Latin family. They all arose from Latin. As Latin spread to different parts of the Roman Empire, and as people moved to different geographical areas within the empire, the way in which different groups spoke Latin came to vary.

English, German, Swedish, Dutch, Danish, Norwegian, and Yiddish (and other languages) are Germanic languages. They all came from the same "mother" language, a language linguists call "Proto-Germanic". Further back in time, both Latin and Proto-Germanic (and other languages) were "daughters" of a common language called "Indo-European". Indo-European itself was a daughter language of a yet earlier language, and so on back to the first language all humans shared at or near the beginning of our evolution as a species.

To a linguist, there is no clear way to sharply distinguish between a dialect and language. Spanish and French could just as easily be considered dialects of Latin as separate languages in their own right. But Latin is gone as a living language, and Spanish and French are spoken in different countries, so political forces kick in and we call them different languages and not dialects of the same language.

Groups who become isolated from an original larger group speak only to their own group members. Since they have lost contact with the others from the original group, they are no longer influenced by them in how they speak and how they change their language.

Geography is not the only way people can become isolated from each other, however. If any group of people ceases communicating with another group, the two groups will eventually diverge in how they speak. They will speak different dialects of a language, or, given enough time, they will speak different languages. People can cease communicating with each other for all sorts of reasons, including geographical distance, hatred, class differences, cultural differences, or religious differences.

If people who speak the same language are segregated by race or class (or by other social or cultural factors) they will speak different dialects, sometimes quite different ones. If they cease to communicate at all, these dialects could diverge into what will eventually be considered separate languages. In the United States, African-Americans spoke a different dialect of English than white people in the past, and some still do today. The same is true of speakers from lower socioeconomic classes and people from higher ones. In any society, there may be dialects based on "race" (races as we construe them do not exist at the biological level) or class, as well as other social divisions such as gender or ethnicity, if these divisions lead to some groups communicating much less or not at all with other groups.

The more people communicate across racial, cultural, or class divides, the more their dialects begin to converge back together into a common language. The less they communicate, the more their dialects stay different and become ever yet more different. If everyone communicated regularly and on equal social terms with everyone else in a society, everyone would eventually speak the same dialect and share in the same changes across time.

Here we see the **principle of language and society**. Language use and variation reflect the structure of, and divisions within, a society or social group. Language both unites and divides us at one and the same time. Note the two different ways to say the same thing below:

1a. We be having left-overs
1b. We have left-overs all the time

(1a) is a so-called "naked *be*" form that is part of the dialect of some African-Americans. It is what linguists call a habitual or durative aspect marker. It means that we have left-overs regularly or habitually. (1b) is from so-called Standard English and means much the same thing, but gains this meaning from the adverb "all the time". Older forms of English had a habitual/durative aspect marker, but Standard English no longer does. The dialect of African-American English, of which (1a) is a part, was influenced by earlier varieties of English and by African languages that African slaves brought with them to America. Here we see that (1a) and (1b) are part of the history of English that both unites and divides us.

Recommended reading

John R. Rickford (1999). *African-American Vernacular English: Features, Evolution, Educational Implications.* Oxford: Blackwell.

1.4 Borrowing

Languages change not just by different groups of speakers becoming isolated from each other: they can also change by borrowing from each other when two or more languages are spoken near each other or even by the same speakers (Grosjean 2010; Weinreich 1953).

English is a good example of borrowing. England was invaded by the Romans in 55 BCE and was converted to Christianity in the 7th century. Both these events caused English to borrow from Latin. England was also invaded by the Normans in 1066. The Normans spoke a version of French, and, in turn, English borrowed from Norman French (a Latinate language, of course). These borrowings left English something of a mixture of Latin and German. Thus, English today differs a good bit from German, even though it is historically, in its origins, a Germanic language. Because of the close connections between Latin and Greek in the Roman Empire, and in the Catholic Church, English also borrowed from Greek (Crystal 2010).

At the level of vocabulary, English has become a sort of dual language. The vocabulary of English is composed of two sets of words, Latinate (and Greek) words and Germanic words. But these words are often used in different contexts.

The Latinate vocabulary is used largely (though not exclusively) in more formal styles of speaking. It is also found in high proportions in academic books and "educated talk". The Germanic vocabulary is used largely (but not exclusively) in less formal styles of speech and in "everyday life". So, for example, consider the two sentences below in which I have bolded words borrowed from Latin:

1. Folks don't all grow up in the same ways.
2. **Human development displays** a **significant amount** of **variation**.

It is almost like these two sentences are in different dialects of English. (1) is totally Germanic. Aside from the little grammatical words like "of", (2) is entirely Latinate. Of course, many instances of informal everyday language use Latinate words that have become common:

3. **People sure** don't all grow up in the same ways.

The divide between Germanic words and Latinate words plays a large role in English in areas such as education, social class, and how we bond with, or show deference for—or distance ourselves from—others. Note that in the examples in Section 2 exemplifying the fast-and-clear principle, the fast version is largely Germanic and the slow one is much more Latinate.

Recommended reading

John McWhorter (2009). *Our Magnificent Bastard Tongue: The Untold History of English*. New York: Random House.

1.5 Social languages

We have seen that languages are always changing, at faster or slower rates, depending on various social factors. They change because individual humans—each of whom is different and unique—learn them and speak them. Each of us speaks our own language (or languages) in our own way, with our own style and idiosyncrasies. We can say that each person has their own "idiolect", their own individual version of a dialect or language they share with others.

Dialects and idiolects are part of language variation. Dialects express regional, class, social, or cultural differences among people. Idiolects express people's individual differences, even within a given group or culture.

There are also other ways language can vary (Labov 1972a, 1972b, 2006; Wolfram & Schilling-Estes 2016). For one, people in any social group or culture vary how they speak in different social settings (different situations or contexts of language use), for example, in more formal situations versus in less formal ones. For another, they can also vary how they speak in terms of the different purposes they have or the specific work they want to use language for. Varieties of a language based on social settings or specific purposes are sometimes called **registers**.

All speakers of any language can speak in more or less formal styles (registers), but they may well use different dialects when they do so. However, in some cases, the most formal varieties in a language may require the use of a certain designated dialect (e.g., "Standard English") for social or political reasons.

Different dialects of English (e.g., Southern American English, British English, Irish English, standard varieties of English used in Africa or India), and even different foreign varieties of English, do not stop physicists from using the register of physics in English, nor do they stop young people, from across the globe, from using the register of *Magic: The Gathering* cards in English (a card game about battles between wizards that works somewhat like *Dungeons and Dragons*). It makes little difference whether a person speaks with an accent or with grammatical anomalies that do not destroy meaning when they "speak" physics or *Magic: The Gathering*. What matters is that they get the register right (i.e., talk or write like a physicist or a *Magic: The Gathering* aficionado). Some registers require more formality—usually because they are used among people who are not kin or friends—than is typical of our everyday talk with people we know well.

There is no one term for all these ways (and others) that language can vary. I will call them all—dialect, idiolects, and registers— **social languages** (Gee 2004). They are all ways that people use language to signal *who* they are to others in different situations.

By "who they are" I mean a **social identity**. Social languages (different styles or varieties of language) are used to place ourselves and others into the social and cultural geography of our society and various social groups within it. A given way of using language—a given dialect, idiolect, or register—"says" to others: "Here and now in this interaction I am X", where X may be a member of a certain class, ethnic group, gender, work group (e.g., doctor, lawyer, linguist, carpenter); interest-based or activity-based group (e.g., a gang member, a *Magic: The Gathering* player, or someone into robotics); or each of us as a socially recognizable individual.

It can happen that when a person uses a certain social language they hear themselves differently than others do. For example, a person from New York could use a dialect that others perceive as "lower socioeconomic New York English"—a class-based dialect—but that person may perceive him or herself as speaking "middle-class English". This sort of thing happens because humans hear themselves differently from how other people hear them. We tend to hear how we speak in terms of what we value, how we aspire to be heard, rather than in terms of how we actually sound to others. This, of course, can lead to problems and complexities.

People can evaluate different varieties of English differently for social and political reasons, reasons that have nothing to do with the linguistic "facts" about how they speak. For example, there are some Americans who devalue Mexican-American English, but admire how a French speaker of English sounds. Yet both varieties are simply influenced by a Romance (Latinate) language. Ironically, English itself has long been partly formed by Latin.

As we have mentioned, each of us has our own idiolect, our own way of using language. Our idiolect says "I am here" even across all the other social identities (e.g., African-American, *Magic: The Gathering* fan, professional engineer, jazz aficionado) a person may have. But this is not "I" as some private asocial person, but as who and how I present myself to others as "me", even across all the different ways I speak and act in different situations.

The idea of social languages—of language variation as a marker of identity—brings us to the **principle of language and identity.** How we use language—how we put different grammatical resources to use in different situations or contexts—is the way we linguistically enact and recognize socially meaningful identities.

Recommended reading

John Edwards (2009). *Language and Identity.* Cambridge: Cambridge University Press.

1.6 Linguists' grammar, prescriptive grammars, and Standard English

By "grammar" we mean a system of rules and principles that exists in the human mind/brain. This system represents what counts as a word, phrase, or sentence in the language and what core meanings these units have. Linguists attempt to describe the properties of a grammar by careful observation of how people talk and how they judge what is grammatical or not in their language or dialect.

By "grammar" I do not mean so-called "prescriptive grammars". Such grammars are written in books and supposedly tell people what is correct or not, based on social conventions and status.

In some African-American dialects of English a sentence like "He be followin' me" (with the so-called "naked be" construction) is fully grammatical. This means that it is used and understood in regular and predicable ways by speakers of this dialect; that they accept it as normal in their dialect; and that it relates to other aspects of their dialect in predicable and logical ways (Bailey & Maynor 1987; Baugh 2000; Rickford & Rickford 2000). Furthermore, this type of construction (which is what linguists call a "habitual/durative aspect marker") is found in many other languages and used to exist in earlier varieties of English.

Prescriptive grammars of English usually tell people how to speak so-called "Standard English". Standard English is the sort of English used (for conventional reasons, not because it is superior to any other dialect) in mainstream public institutions, media, and encounters. Standard English varies in the USA, England, Scotland, New Zealand, and Australia (and other countries that have standard varieties of English, including some in Africa and India).

Standard English has its historical origins in 14th-century London. London had become the political and commercial center of England by then. People from all over the country moved to London, or were influenced by London. For those who wished to achieve status and influence, speaking London English was becoming a necessity. Thus, this regional dialect gained national prestige and standing. If the political and commercial center had been somewhere else, another dialect would have taken its place as a public and national standard (Wright 2000).

Standard English is in many ways not so much a dialect of English as it is a social and conventional "ideal" toward which some people aim when they are being more formal, but which in their day-to-day talk they reflect only in part amidst much variation.

Recommended reading

James Milroy and Leslie Milroy (2012). *Authority in Language: Investigating Standard English.* Third Edition. New York: Routledge.

References

Aitchison, J. (2001). *Language Change: Progress or Decay?* Third Edition. Cambridge: Cambridge University Press.

Bailey, G. & Maynor, N. (1987). Decreolization. *Language in Society* 16: 449–473.

Baugh, J. (2000). *Beyond Ebonics: Linguistic Pride and Racial Prejudice.* New York: Oxford University Press.

Coulmas, F. & Watts, R. J. (2006). *Sociolinguistics: The Study of Speaker's Choices.* Cambridge: Cambridge University Press.

Crystal, D. (2010). *Cambridge Encyclopedia of the English Language.* Third Edition. Cambridge: Cambridge University Press.

Gee, J. P. (2004). *Situated Language and Learning: A Critique of Traditional Schooling.* London: Routledge.

Grosjean, F. (2010). *Bilingual: Life and Reality.* Cambridge, MA: Harvard University Press.

Labov, W. (1972a). *Language in the Inner City: Studies in Black English Vernacular.* Philadelphia, PA: University of Pennsylvania Press.

Labov, W. (1972b). *Sociolinguistic Patterns.* Philadelphia, PA: University of Pennsylvania Press.

Labov, W. (2006). *Principles of Linguistic Change: Synthesis.* Oxford: Blackwell.

Pinker, S. (1994). *The Language Instinct: How the Mind Creates Language.* New York: HarperCollins.

Rickford, J. R. & Rickford, R. J. (2000). *Spoken Soul: The Story of Black English*. New York: John Wiley & Sons.

Safina, C. (2015). *Beyond Words: What Animals Think and Feel*. New York: Henry Holt.

Slobin, D. I. (1977). Language Change in Childhood and History. In J. Macnamara, Ed., *Language Learning and Thought*. New York: Academic Press, pp. 185–214.

Weinreich, W. (1953). *Languages in Contact*. The Hague: Mouton & Co.

Wolfram, W. & Schilling-Estes, N. (2016). *American English: Dialects and Variation*. Third Edition. Malden, MA: Wiley.

Wright, L., Ed. (2000). *The Development of Standard English, 1300–1800: Theories, Descriptions, Conflicts*. Cambridge: Cambridge University Press.

2

System and situation

2.1 Grammar

The **grammar** of any human language is composed of different systems: the **lexicon** (words), **syntax** (structure), and **semantics** (meaning). Grammar is a system (like algebra, a cell, the immune system, or the solar system) in the sense that it is a complex whole, made up of connected and interacting parts, a whole that is more than the sum of its parts. It is like natural systems in that no human being designed it. It arose as part of human biology and the evolution of the human brain.

At the same time, grammar is social in the sense that it is like a game (a very complex one) that is played by rules (social conventions). So, grammar also arose as part of human history and as part of the process of the invention and evolution of culture.

The word "lexicon" is used by linguists to mean the "dictionary" we have in our heads, that is, the words we know and their basic meanings. In our mental lexicon, words are associated with their pronunciation; with their structure in terms of **morphemes** (meaningful sub-parts of a word as in "un-faith-ful" or "un-know-able"); and with what we will call **core meaning** (**semantics**). Core meaning is the literal or basic meaning of a word when we consider it out of any specific context of use.

Syntax is a system made up of rules (principles, procedures) that determine how different categories of words (nouns, verbs, adjectives, adverbs, and function words such as "the" or "of") can combine into phrases and then into clauses and sentences. These rules are stored in our heads, but are also part of social conventions we share with the other speakers of our language or languages.

In English, nouns are the heads (main element) of noun phrases; verbs are the heads of verb phrases; adjectives are the heads of adjective phrases; adverbs are the heads of adverb phrases; and prepositions are the heads of prepositional phrases:

1a. **destruction** (noun)
1b. the complete **destruction** of the Roman Empire (noun phrase)

2a. **destroy** (verb)
2b. completely **destroy** the Roman Empire (verb phrase)

3a. **destructive** (adjective)
3b. violently **destructive** by historical standards (adjective phrase)

4a. **quickly** (adverb)
4b. (he ran) quite **quickly** at first (adverb phrase)

5a. **inside** (preposition)
5b. completely **inside** the box (prepositional phrase)

> **Note 1**: Traditional grammar uses the term "adverb phrase" in a different way than I do here. Traditional grammar treats any phrase that modifies a verb as an adverb phrase. So "wisely" in "She spoke wisely" is an adverb and "with wisdom" in "She spoke with wisdom" is an adverb phrase because it is a group of words that modifies the verb ("speak") in much the same way that "wisely" does. In this book, "wisely" is an adverb (and "quite wisely" is an adverbial phrase), but "with wisdom" is a prepositional phrase, since its head (the word it is organized around) is the preposition "with".

> **Note 2:** To save words linguists often call both a single noun (as in "**Girls** like video games" and a noun accompanied by other words (as in "**The girls from school** like video games") noun phrases. They use the same terminology for verbs, adjectives, adverbs, and prepositions).

Clauses and sentences are composed of a **subject**, which serves as a **topic**, a main verb (that can be accompanied by helping verbs and adverbs), and any material that follows the verb. The verb (with its adverbs and helping verbs) and any material following it is called the **predicate**. The predicate serves as the **comment** on the subject/topic:

Sentence: The violent destruction of the Roman Empire (**subject/topic**) destroyed (**main verb**) all hope for peace (**predicate/comment**)

Sentence:

Clause 1: When the woman (**subject/topic**)

left (**main verb/predicate/comment**)

Clause 2: She (**subject/topic**)

really traveled (**main verb**) very far from home (**predicate/comment**)

Note that in a sentence like "In the afternoon, John went shopping with his sister", "John" is the subject/topic and "went shopping with his sister" is the predicate/comment. "In the afternoon" is an adjunct that modifies "John went shopping with his sister" (tells us when this happened).

In "John went shopping with his sister in the afternoon", "John" is the subject/topic and "went shopping with his sister in the afternoon" is the predicate/comment. "In the afternoon" still modifies "John went shopping with his sister", but now it is also a part of the predicate, since it follows the main verb ("went"). Such adjuncts can move fairly freely around a clause or sentence: "In the summer, Mary always plants tulips; "Mary, in the summer, always plants tulips"; "Mary always plants tulips in the summer".

Semantics is the part of the linguistic system concerned with what we have called **core meaning**. Each word in a language has a core meaning. Thus, "cat" means a member of the feline species. "Democracy" means a system of government based on voting and representation. "Bachelor" means an unmarried male. Core meaning is the basic literal meaning a word has when we consider it out of any specific context of use.

Since syntax tells us what sorts of words can combine with other words to make up phrases, it also tells us what groups of words need to be assigned core meanings together. Semantic rules tell us what these meanings are.

So, for example, "gray" means the color gray and "elephant" means a specific species of mammal. The combination (phrase) "a gray elephant" means something that is both gray and an elephant.

On the other hand, "small" means not big or tall and elephant means a specific species of mammal. Thus, if "small elephant" worked like "gray elephant" we would expect the phrase "a small elephant" to be mean something that is both small and an elephant. But there are no elephants that aren't big things. The phrase "a small elephant" means "something that is small *for an elephant*". That is why we can talk about "big mice", though all mice are always small as animals go (big mice are mice that are big in comparison to average mice).

What we see here is that the syntactic pattern "adjective noun" (gray elephant, small elephant) falls into two different semantic patterns (there are others as well):

1a. **Pattern 1**

    adjective + noun means: both Adjective and Noun

        gray + elephant means: both gray and elephant

1b. **Pattern 2**

    adjective + noun means: adjective for a noun

        small + elephant means: small for an elephant

A note on grammars

There are many good modern traditional grammars of English, but, to my mind, still none better that Otto Jespersen's work, which has long set the standard for grammatical description:

Otto Jespersen (1924). *The Philosophy of Grammar*. London: George Allen & Unwin. 1992 Edition with an Introduction by James D. McCawley. Chicago, IL: University of Chicago Press.

Otto Jespersen (1933). *Essentials of English Grammar*. New York: George Allen & Unwin. Reprinted 1994, 2002. New York: Routledge.

M. A. Halliday's functional grammar (a grammar that relates structure to function) is the best known functional grammar and often used in discourse analysis. It is best to start with a secondary source (see Thompson below), though, since Halliday's approach is quite different from traditional grammars:

Michael A. Halliday (2013). *Halliday's Introduction to Functional Grammar*. Fourth Edition. Revised by Christian M. I. M. Matthiessen. New York: Routledge.

Christian Matthiessen, James R. Martin, and Clare Painter (1996). *Working with Functional Grammar*. London: Routledge.

Geoff Thompson (2014). *Introducing Functional Grammar*. Third Edition. New York: Routledge.

The grammar below is a superb reference work:

Randolph Quirk, Sidney Greenbaum, Geoffrey Leech, and Jan Svartvik (1985). *A Comprehensive Grammar of the English Language.* Second Revised Edition. New York: Longman.

Noam Chomsky's generative grammar is the best-known theoretical approach to the core mental (and biological) properties of the grammar of any natural language. The first book below is accessible to people without formal training in generative linguistics, the second is not, and the third is in-between.

Robert C. Berwick and Noam Chomsky (2015). *Why Only Us: Language and Evolution.* Cambridge, MA: MIT Press.
Noam Chomsky (1995). *The Minimalist Program.* Cambridge, MA: MIT Press.
Noam Chomsky (2002). *On the Nature of Language.* Cambridge: Cambridge University Press.

2.2 Discourse and pragmatics

Discourse is the system that tells us how to use and understand language in specific contexts or situations of use (Brown G. & Yule 1983). Grammar is language as a **system** that exists in the human head, whether or not it is being put to use. However, when grammar is put to use (expressed outwardly), it takes on a great many more properties than those present in grammar as a mental system. Grammar enables these other properties, but these other properties go far beyond grammar itself.

For example, consider a line from e. e. cummings' poem "anyone lived in a pretty how town":"with up so many floating bells down". Cummings' poem is an actual use of language. It breaks many rules of English grammar and that is part of how the poem achieves certain sorts of effects on its readers. But note that these effects would not be possible without grammar—otherwise we would have no idea cummings was breaking the rules and no basis on which to ask why (which is, by the way, the beginning of doing a discourse analysis).

It is sometimes said that discourse is the level "above" grammar in the sense that grammar tells us what counts as a grammatical sentence and discourse tells us how to string sentences together into larger stretches of speech or writing. When linguists use the word "discourse" in this way, they tend to define discourse analysis as the analysis of language beyond the sentence level. In turn, they call the study of language in use (how people interpret spoken and written language in actual situations of use) "pragmatics".

I interpret discourse analysis to mean the study of how language is constructed beyond the sentence level *and* how language (whether a single word or sentence or longer) works (is used and interpreted) in specific situations of use in the contexts of social interactions, institutions, and social and cultural groups. Thus, I dispense with the term "pragmatics", but do note that work published under the labels "discourse analysis" or "pragmatics" is relevant to our concerns.

The distinction and relationship between system (core system) and situation (language in use) is much like those between a tool and its use. A hammer has a certain design (a "grammar") and that design strongly suggests some of the hammer's possibilities (affordances). But the design does not by any means determine all the uses that can be made of the hammer. While we can use it to hammer things (the use its design suggests and affords), we can also use it as a weapon, a doorstop, a paper weight, a digging tool, and many other things. We can't use it for everything, however—and its core design determines that as well. You cannot use a hammer as food or as a telescope. There are limits.

Recommended reading:

Stephen Levinson (1983). *Pragmatics*. Cambridge: Cambridge University Press.

2.3 Grammar and perspectives

The lexicon (words), syntax (structure), and semantics (core meaning) together make up grammar. Grammar constitutes a theory of (a set of perspectives on) what can be thought and said. While the grammar of our language guides our thoughts and claims about the world—and the grammars of different languages do so differently—it does not determine the limits of what we can think and say (Agar 1994; Whorf 1956).

Nonetheless, the grammar of our language tends to determine our initial way of thinking and talking about things unless problems arise that make us think more consciously about how to view things. When we are exposed to new languages or new cultures we may face problems or have insights that allow us eventually to think and talk in new ways, even in our native language.

Many of us were taught in school that nouns name persons, places, or things; that verbs name actions or processes; and that adjectives name attributes (properties) or states. But this is not true. In English, in many cases, one and the same word can be used as a noun, verb, adjective, or even adverb:

1a. The hurricane **destroyed** (verb) the city in 1992
1b. The **destruction** (noun) of the city by a hurricane in 1992
1c. The **destructive** (adjective) forces of the 1992 hurricane
1d. The hurricane moved **destructively** (adverb) along the coast in 1992

2a. The old man **died** (verb)
2b. The old man's **death** (noun)
2c. The old man is **dead** (adjective)
2d. The old man was dealt a **deadly** (adverb) blow to the head

3a. Mary **loved** (verb) Juan
3b. Mary's **love** (noun) for Juan
3c. Mary's touch is a **loving** (adjective) force
3d. Mary touched Juan **lovingly** (adverb)

4. We **honored** (verb) the **honorable** (adjective) senator's sense of **honor** (noun) **honorably** (adverb)

Semantics gives words core meanings (in the lexicon) and gives phrases and sentences core meanings by combining word meanings to make up phrase meanings and phrase meanings to make up clause and sentence meanings, using syntax as a guide. Core meanings are not about reality. They are about **perspectives** on reality.

(1a) views the destruction as an **action** (destroy) carried out by an actor or force (the hurricane). (1b) views it as a **thing** or **event** that happened at one time and place (destruction in 1992). (1c) views it as an **attribute** of the hurricane's forces (destructive). 1(d) views it as an **attribute** (property) of the hurricane's movement (destructively).

What is destroy/destruction/destructive/destructively "really" in the world? In reality, if we take a long enough temporal perspective, everything in the world is a process, since everything is changing, however imperceptibly, at every moment. Grammar does not care about this and allows us to talk about destruction in different ways, to take different perspectives on it.

It is hard for us humans to view some things in multiple ways. Something like a mountain—though in reality it changes through time and so, in a large view over lots of time, could be seen as a process—is so stable in the short run that it is hard to view it as anything other than a thing. But imagine a creature that lived for millions of years and, thus saw mountains arise, grow, and then erode away. Such a creature might say things, in English, like "It **mountained** (verb) over there for 250,000 years, but is no longer"; "It is starting to **mountain** (verb) here"; "That was a **mountainy** (adjective) time for this region". And, after all, even us short-lived creatures can say "That area of the country is **mountainous** (adjective)".

Different languages differ in the perspectives they take on the world. Some languages have only two basic color terms (for light and dark) and some have three or more, up to about 11 basic terms (Berlin & Kay 1991). English distinguishes between "loving" and "liking" and so can say something like: "I love Mary and I like Sue", where French would use the same verb for both: "J'aime Mary et j'aime Sue". English allows things that helped cause something to happen—but which are not animate agents—to be the subjects of sentences, as in "The rock broke the window", while Jacaltec, a Mayan language, insists that subjects of transitive verbs must be animate agents (Becker 2014).

Recommended reading

Clare Kramsch (1998). *Language and Culture*. Oxford: Oxford University Press.

2.4 Grammatical patterns and perspectives

We have argued that grammar (words, syntax, and semantics) gives us perspectives on what there is to think about and talk about and how to do so. Grammar is full of **patterns** (constructions) that offer us ways to take different perspectives, often on the same thing. Different grammatical patterns are associated with different perspectival meanings. So, consider the pattern below:

Locator pattern

1a. John is standing next to the fountain
1b. John is next to the fountain

2a. John is sitting in the armchair
2b. John is in the armchair

3a. John finished 4th in the race
3b. John was 4th in the race

4a. John placed in the 90% percentile on the SAT
4b. John is in the 90% percentile on the SAT

5a. John was assigned to be the reporter
5b. John is the reporter

This grammatical pattern allows speakers two different ways to look at placing people in regard to something else. The (a) sentences use an action or a process (e.g., "placed") to locate John (e.g., "in the 90th percentile") in regard to some reference point (e.g., the SAT). The (b) sentences locate John by assigning him an attribute of being in some position in regard to a reference point ("is in the 90th percentile on the SAT"), leaving aside the action or process that got him there. This attribute is not a property of John *per se*, but is a joint property of John and a reference point, it is a relationship between two things (John and an SAT score).

Here is another grammatical pattern associated with a different set of perspectives:

Personal property pattern

1a. John is a tall person
1b. John is tall

2a. John is a cautious person
2b. John is cautious

3a. John is an African–American (person)
3b. John is African–American

4a. John is an honorable person
4b. John is honorable

This pattern allows speakers to take two different perspectives on the attributes of people. The (a) sentences attribute being a certain type of person (e.g., "a cautious person") to John, they locate him in a particular group or set of people (cautious people). The (b) sentences attribute to John the property ("is cautious") that defines the group. Unlike in the case of the locator pattern sentences (e.g., "John is next to the fountain") the (b) sentences here state attributes that are "inherent" (individual) properties of John *per se*.

Now consider the following two sentences:

1a. John scored a 3 on the English as a Second Language Test
1b. John is a 3 on the English as a Second Language Test

These two sentences are obviously in the locator pattern. They locate John in reference to scores on a test. (1a) does so in regard to an action (score) and the second in regard to a relation between John and a test score.

2.5 Category errors

There is a test in my home state (Arizona) that scores immigrant students 1 through 4 on their knowledge of English as a second language. The students are then taken out of their regular content courses and placed in special English language literacy classes based on this score. Thus, they miss out on academic content while being drilled on English literacy. Below is a transcript of some teachers who teach these special classes talking with a researcher (Amy) about their English as a Second Language (ESL) students (data from—and thanks to—Amy J. Heinke, *Teachers' Discourse on English Language Learners: Cultural Models of Language and Learning*, Unpublished doctoral dissertation, College of Education, Arizona State University, Tempe, Arizona):

Erica: But I think that I've probably seen this difference [linguistic] because I [my classroom] am the mix, I have threes and fours, so I can see like those [students] who—and I have some threes that I swear could be fours, I don't think they're three.

Amy: What do you see as the distinction between [a three and four]?

Erica: Like they learn, well, I won't say they learn things faster, but they do seem to pick up a little faster, and then their output [spoken English] is so different.

Joni: Between a four and a three? Yeah.

Erica: Oh, yes. Like the output is different. Like they're the kind of kids that will take the language objectives and remember to use it, they are the ones that are a little bit more self-initiated. They will try to read, if you say point to the words and follow me, they will, these are seen as differences between a three and a four.

Joni: My home base is fours, and I mean, they rock, most of my kids rock

Something very interesting—but not uncommon—is happening here. A claim that a child is a 3, which is a claim that follows the locator pattern, is (through talk and interaction) coming to be treated as if it were in the personal property pattern.

The locator pattern treats a claim like "this child is a 3" as a statement about the child's location within a set of test scores. It states a relationship between the child and something outside the child (a test score). However, the teachers are sliding towards treating the test score as defining the child as a type of person and then attributing to the child the defining properties (whatever they might be) of that type (which would fit the personal property pattern). The problem is that no one knows what the defining properties are of the "kind of person" who scores 3 on the test. This kind does not actually exist (yet). So, the teachers are seeking to discover such properties (e.g., "self-initiated", a property that might, in fact, have little to do with how much English one knows).

Enough of this sort of talk and "Johnnie is a 3" will come to mean Johnnie is the type of person who is a 3 and the property or properties that make someone that kind of person will be seen as inherent properties of Johnnie. It will no longer just mean Johnnie scored 3 on the test.

The teachers are beginning to make a category error. They are treating the category of *student-score pairings* (a relational property) as a category of *kinds of people* and, thus, internal or inherent traits of people. Why are they doing this? They are doing it because of how they have been placed in relation to their students by policies and institutions of which they must make sense.

Unfortunately, placing external attributes inside people is all too common among us humans, especially when we have to make interactional sense of a situation that we find perplexing. However, once policies, institutions, talk, and texts have done their work, this category error will begin to function as a "reality" in the world with real consequences. One consequence would be the perspective that some children because of *who* they *are* need to be taken out of their content classes (no matter whatever loss in learning this might incur and no matter how well learning content initially in their home language might have worked) and taught English language literacy.

Note, too, that the researcher's question ("What do you see as the distinction between a three and a four?") has two different possible meanings: What do you see as the distinction between a three and a four on the test? (which is a question about how a person's placement on the test is determined) and What do you see as the distinction between a three person and a four person? (which is squarely in the personal property pattern and invites the teachers to treat the test scores as indicators of kinds of people with specific personal attributes).

This example of children becoming "kinds of people" based on a test score (which can somehow discover or uncover that kind), rather than just names on a paired list of students and scores, is a good example of how language as a system (grammar) interacts with situational meaning (meanings we make up in actual uses of language). The grammatical construction "Johnnie scored 3 on the test" → "Johnnie is a 3 on the test" has conventional meaning built into the grammar of English: *Johnnie is located at 3 on the test*. But, as we have seen, people can change language. People can start giving a new meaning in actual situations of use to "Johnnie is 3". This is a situational meaning, an extension to core meaning. If this way of using "Johnnie is 3" and claims like it spread widely, it could, in the end, change core meaning; tests scores could leave the locator pattern and join the personal property pattern.

2.6 More perspectival grammatical patterns

As we have said, grammar offers speakers a theory (a set of perspectives) on how to think and talk about things. These perspectives are not necessarily "true". They arose as part of human evolution and language change through history. We humans certainly can come up with perspectives that are counter to what the grammar of our languages suggest, but we have to think consciously, reflectively, and critically to do so (Goldberg 1995; Hoffman & Trousdale 2013; Tomasello 2003)

Consider the following grammatical pattern as an example:

1a. Mary handed John a book
1b. Mary handed a book to John

2a. Mary sent John a message
2b. Mary sent a message to John

3a. Mary gave John hope
3b. Mary gave hope to John

4a. Mary gave John her cold
4b. Mary gave her cold to John

5a. Mary taught the students biology
5b. Mary taught biology to the students

This is what we can call the **transfer pattern**. It gives speakers two different ways to say that something went from one place to another place. Note the "thing" that moves does not have to be a physical thing.

(5a–b) suggest, then, that teaching is the transfer of something from one person to another. Interestingly enough, the ancient Greek philosopher Socrates held a very different view of teaching. For Socrates, teachers did not put knowledge *into* students, but *drew it out* of them, knowledge that was already inside them without their consciously knowing it. Thus, in Plato's dialogue *Meno* (402 BCE), Socrates demonstrates that a slave boy already knows mathematics and just needs a teacher (Socrates, in this case) to draw it out of him (to render the slave boy's knowledge conscious). The Latin root of our word "educate" means "to lead out", "to lead forth", a view closer to Socrates' view than to the one suggested by our current grammar.

Now compare the following pairs of sentences:

6a. Mary taught the students biology/taught biology to the students
6b. Mary taught the students how to do biology

7a. Mary taught the kids cooking/taught cooking to the kids
7b. Mary taught the kids to cook

(6a) and (7a) treat biology and cooking as things ("content" of some form) that can be transferred. (6b) and (7b) treat biology and cooking as actions or skills. A word like "biology" or "cooking" can mean either a body of knowledge or the actions, practices, and skills that generate that knowledge. The ways of speaking in (6a) and (7a) make biology and cooking sound like "subject matter" (though we could interpret them differently if we want), while the ways of speaking in (6b) and (7b) make biology and cooking sound like activities.

We can note that the idiom in (6a) is far more common than the one in (6b) when we are talking about typical school subjects, but the idiom in (7b) is more common than the one in (7a) when we are talking about teaching and learning out of school. Thus, note that something like "John taught the other kids to play video games" is far more common than something like

"John taught the other kids video gaming/taught video gaming to the kids" (though this might change if we made gaming a school subject).

Recommended reading

Adele A. Goldberg (2006). *Constructions at Work: The Nature of Generalization in Language*. Oxford: Oxford University Press.

2.7 Grammatical patterns, perspectives, and metaphors

A sentence like "Mary gave them hope" is basically a metaphor. "Hope" is not something that can literally be transferred like a book or even a cold. The grammars of all languages "bake in" certain metaphorical or figurative ways of looking at the world (Bergen 2012; Lakoff 1987). Some of these metaphorical ways of looking at the world are common across many or all languages and some are not and reside in only one or a few languages. Such "baked in" metaphors are an important way in which grammars express their theories of what can be thought and said.

For example, the verb "see" has a core meaning of physically sighting something, but we regularly use it as well to mean seeing things that are not actually visible, as in "I see your point", "I don't see what you are getting at", or "I can't see any good in what you are doing". This extended metaphorical use is not novel, but common to English daily expression and very much part of the core meaning of sentence like "I saw his point".

Here are just a very few of the metaphors (the (b) sentences below) that are built into the grammar of English. Since they are built into grammar, many speakers are unaware they are metaphorical when they use them:

1a. He lost his keys
1b. He lost his mind

2a. He came back home
2b. He came back to his senses

3a. I defeated John in boxing
3b. I defeated my fears

4a. She couldn't keep the kitten in the box
4b. She couldn't keep the idea in her head

5a. I lost my keys
5b. I lost my motivation

6a. She went out of the house
6b. She went out of her mind

7a. John is standing by his wife in the photo
7b. John is standing by his wife in her time of need

English often organizes whole domains in terms of a set of related metaphors. For example, English regularly treats argument as warfare, that is, it
uses terms for warfare to talk about argument (though, of course, there are
other ways to talk about argument):

8a. His claims were *indefensible* and easy to *defeat*
8b. She *attacked* every point in my argument until I *gave up*
8c. His sharp-edged criticisms were right on *target*
8d. She thoroughly *demolished* my argument
8e. She thoroughly *demolished* me
8f. He *shot* down all my arguments
8g. The *war of words* between the two candidates got hot in last night's debate

English does much the same for romance and love:

9a. She *fought* for his love, but his old girlfriend *won* in the end
9b. I am slowly *gaining ground* on her *emotional defenses,* but it's an uphill
battle
9c. He *won* her hand in marriage
9d. She is utterly *besieged* by suitors
9e. She has to *fend off* many men's attentions
9f. He is working hard to make a loyal *ally* of her mother
9g. She is known and admired for her many *conquests* and all the men she
subdued
9h. She *surrendered* her virginity to her more *forceful* suitor

English treats relationships also in terms of money metaphors about investing:

10a. She *invested* a lot of time and effort in the relationship
10b. He *earned* her hand in marriage
10c. The *rewards* of marriage are great
10d. She did not *get out* of it what she had *put into* it

10e. Their *mutual investment* in their marriage *paid off*

10f. We have *invested* a lot of time and resources into our children

10g. I've *invested* too much in this marriage to leave it now

English also uses money metaphors for time:

11a. That was time *well spent*

11b. You are *wasting* my time

11c. I *invested* a lot of time in the effort

11d. I *saved* time doing it that way

11e. I *earned* more vacation time

11f. Time is *money*

11g. I *lost* time on the test by not guessing

11h. I try to *budget* my time

Finally, note that English treats the head/brain as a container into and out of which things can go:

12a. I finally got the point into his head

12b. I just could not keep the information in my head

12c. I *lost my train of thought*

12d. *Keep in mind* that that is the way things are here

12e. He has lots of facts *in his head*, but no wisdom

12f. I can't get you *out of my head*

12g. That song is *stuck in my head*

Such metaphorical systems, built into the grammars of our languages, shape how we talk and think, especially when we are not critically and consciously investigating things. One of the reasons people in specialist domains, whether academic areas such as physics or non-academic ones such as video gaming, make up new word meanings, new metaphors, and new ways of speaking is that they want to change how everyday language makes us think and talk about things. That is what Socrates did when instead of saying (in Greek of course) "The teacher taught the student mathematics" he said "The teacher drew mathematics out of the student".

We could also substitute things like "The teacher energized her students to learn mathematics" or "The teacher scaffolded the students' mathematics learning" (using a technical term from education) instead of "The teacher taught mathematics" if we wanted to push another perspective on teaching. The point is not which perspectives are "right", but where they come from and how much we have actually thought about them. After all, when we teach, nothing is "really" transferred (moved) from one person to another and nothing is put "into" people's brains, since brains are not "really" boxes. If you give a book to someone else you no longer have the book, but if you give them knowledge or know-how you still have them, much like giving someone love.

Recommended reading

George Lakoff and Mark Johnson (1980). *Metaphors We Live By*. Chicago, IL: University of Chicago Press.

2.8 Core meanings and situational meanings

Words, as we have said, have core meanings (semantics). A core meaning represents what we will call the **meaning potential** of a word. Core meaning is something around which people can "riff" in actual language use, guiding the potential for extensions and nuances of all sorts.

So, as an example, take the word "coffee". The core meaning of this word is something like "a drink made from ground seeds of a specific sort of plant" (a bush, but most of us have no real idea what the actual plant is, other than the one we somehow get coffee from). This basic meaning just gives us a central focus around which, in use, we can give the word different, more specific and nuanced, and sometimes even innovative, meanings. We call these meanings **situational meanings**. Here are some examples of different situational meanings for the word "coffee":

1a. The coffee (liquid) spilled, go get a mop and clean it up
1b. The coffee (grains or beans) spilled, go get a broom and clean it up
1c. The coffee (cans of coffee) spilled, go stack it again
1d. I pick coffee (berries on a plant) for a living
1e. I want a scoop of coffee (ice-cream)
1f. Big Coffee (the coffee business) is as bad as Big Oil

We do not know how core meanings are stored in the head. They may be like definitions written in a mental language, images, paradigmatic (typical) examples, or networks of associations among words, or some combination of these. The core meanings of words are part of grammar.

A word seeks to name something with boundaries, because some sort of demarcation of a thing or process is necessary if we are to know what we are thinking and talking about. But when we put words to actual uses we face two essential problems. The first problem I will call the **boundary problem** and the second I will call the **identity problem**.

A river is a wide channel of flowing fresh water and a creek is a smaller, narrower channel of flowing fresh water (these are core meanings). But when we go to apply these words in actual situations we are faced with the issue of just how big and wide a flowing channel of water must be to be considered a river.

The Verde River in northern Arizona, which flows behind my farm, is narrow enough at some points that it looks like a creek and wide enough at others that it looks like a river. Should we just call it everywhere a river because it is named the "Verde River" and used to be big everywhere before humans started to use it for irrigation and other uses? If the whole thing became narrow would we/should we rename it as a creek? People near me call it a creek, though they use the name "the Verde River" for the whole thing. Are they wrong? Who gets to determine this? This is the boundary problem and this problem can and often does arise in practice (use) with a great many words. Sometimes, of course, scientists and specialists of other sorts specify (stipulate) in more detail what separates one thing (like a river) from another (like a creek).

The identity problem is this: When does a thing or process cease to be what it is or was? How polluted does a river or creek need to be before it is no longer a body of flowing fresh water? What about when it is so polluted that we can set it on fire with a match? How long does a creek have to be to be a creek? How fast does a creek or river have to flow to be a creek or a river? Obviously, the boundary problem and the identity problem are two sides of the same coin.

In reality, boundaries between categories are often fuzzy and what a thing "really" is can be contested. In the case of creeks and rivers, the issues are usually not all that important (but in the age of water wars and contested water rights they can become so). But issues over the boundaries between human races (say), or whether races are real, have been historically vexed and violent. And, of course, new discoveries can make things that were not all that controversial quite controversial. We now know that "male/female" is not actually a binary division with a clear boundary. We have not entirely changed how we think and speak yet (i.e., what words we use and what they mean), but eventually we very well may.

Because language in use always gives words meanings that are more specific, more nuanced, extended, narrowed, broadened, or newer than their core meanings, many scholars have wanted to argue that there are no such things as core meanings, only meanings in use (situational meanings). But if we didn't start from some shared conception of the "target" (what we wanted to talk about and maybe even contest over) we could not discuss and contest at all.

Recommended reading

Stephen C. Levinson (2000). *Presumptive Meanings: The Theory of Generalized Conversational Implicature.* Cambridge, MA: MIT Press.

2.9 Sausage

Even core meanings that seem sharply bounded—that seem to capture the essence of something—do not. Core meaning (whether given by images, features, examples, or definitions) can only capture a more or less well-bounded range of possibilities.

For example, while a definition like "a bachelor is an unmarried male" seems pretty definitive, the Pope is an unmarried male, but not often referred to as a "bachelor". For words like "democracy" and "sausage" all bets are off about their semantics being rigidly definitive in the sense of defining necessary and sufficient conditions for something being a democracy or sausage in the world. All core meaning can do is state meaning potential and then people put that potential to more nuanced and sometimes creative use in practice (actual language use).

Situational meanings are the meanings people actually give to a word in situations of use, based on their core meanings and the specific demands and features of the situation. By the way, over time, situational meanings can change the range of possible applications for a word and, thus, its core meaning.

In giving a word a situational meaning, speakers must judge whether a thing or event, in an actual situation of use, is sufficiently like the core exemplars or features in the word's core meaning to merit applying the word. How are such judgements made? Let's take, as an example case, the word "sausage" (Williams 1991). You can readily think of all sorts of exemplars of sausage. Or you can just say that sausage is ground up meat parts, together with other ingredients, usually stuffed inside a casing of some sort. This is the semantic meaning (core meaning) for "sausage".

Now, at the food store, you confront applications of the word "sausage" on packages, ads, and in your own talk and decisions. And, alas, there are lots and lots of different things in sausage. All sorts of animal body parts, some of which many people (and some government agencies) don't consider "meat". Here are just a few of the things, other than meat, that can be in sausage: animal fat, rusk, bread crumbs, cereal, water, polyphosphates, soya, colors, preservatives, sulphites, nitrates, antioxidants, flavor enhancers (e.g., monosodium glutamate), and, of course, a wide variety of contaminates.

US government regulations define meat in such a way that pork sausage, for example, can contain up to 30% fat and 25% connective tissue, and lots of other ingredients that no one thinks are meat, and still count both as "meat" and "sausage". On the other hand, some consumers would beg to disagree.

So, consumers, producers, supermarkets, economic markets, government agencies, courts, health groups, and others discuss, contest, and negotiate over what can be said to be "sausage" in actual situations. Consumers do not want sausage to be so "pure" that it is too expensive to buy. Producers want it not so "impure" that consumers die from eating it (because then they can't buy it again), but not so pure and expensive that they cannot sell it. Supermarkets want to keep their customers, but not go broke. Courts are asked things like: "Just how many rat droppings must sausage have in it not to count as sausage anymore"? And people from different cooking cultures have different opinions about what can or cannot be in "real" sausage.

All sorts of people, institutions, interests, and groups get involved and help move situational meanings in different directions through their talk, arguments, actions, interactions, purchases, and cooking. Semantics settles nothing on its own here. Things change. Some people win and some people lose and this changes, too, across time. Situational meaning is social and cultural and contestable and practical, even if people share the same semantics or language.

As far as I know, no one has gone to war over what is in sausage; however, plenty of people have killed, maimed, and gone to war over what "democracy", "Christianity", "Islam", "white", "black", "fair", "just", "liberal", "kin", "family", "God", "honor", "clean", "pure", "male", "female", "reason", "religion", "science", and many other such words—all as messy as sausage—mean or ought to mean at the point of contextual applications to the world.

It is interesting to note that, scientifically, tomatoes are a fruit (because they have seeds), but in 1983 the Supreme Court of the United States ruled they were a vegetable (*Nix v. Hedden*). At the time, there were taxes on imported vegetables, but not fruit. Tomato importers wanted to have tomatoes classified as fruit so that they did not have to pay the tax. The

Supreme Court ruled that, despite what science says, tomatoes count as vegetables in people's everyday language. So, taxes were in order. By the way, tomatoes also count as vegetables in the language of cooks (since they are not sweet).

2.10 Semantics and discourse

That meaning-in-use goes beyond core meaning is normal and ever present. Any time we use a word or phrase, we must customize its meaning to the context or situation in which we are communicating. We can narrow, broaden, extend, or otherwise modify the core meaning of the word or phrase. A word like "terrorist" (core meaning = a person who uses violence against civilians to win their submission) applies differently in different contexts. It is often used in specific contexts to mean people who use violence against civilians in a cause the speaker does not like. Thus, some Americans considered the Mujahideen "freedom fighters" when they were fighting the Russians (our enemies at the time) in Afghanistan, but called the same people "terrorists" later when they were fighting the United States there.

Grammar is only a guide; speakers and writers can creatively (sometimes with good results for others, sometimes not) extend and recreate meaning in actual situations of use. We have called such meaning **situational meanings**.

When we speak or write, we customize or situate basic meanings to the actual contexts or situations in which we are communicating. In this sense, language in use is a creative act. Sometimes, how we create situational meanings is quite novel and sometimes it is fairly routine or no real deviation from core meaning. There is actually a continuum here between highly novel meaning creations and very routinized (taken-for-granted, nearly everyone does it) meanings.

As discourse analysts, we are concerned with situational meanings and how far or in what ways, and for what reasons, they have varied from core meanings in a given situation of language use in which we are interested. Consider below the different uses of the word "democracy", a word whose core meaning has to do with voting and representation:

1a. … yet I believe [Milton] Friedman is right that thoroughgoing restrictions on economic freedom would turn out to be inconsistent with **democracy**.

(Becker and Posner 2006)

1b. Penalosa [Mayor of Bogota, Colombia] observes that "high quality public pedestrian space in general and parks in particular are evidence of true **democracy** at work"
(Brown, L. R. 2008, p. 193).

1c. That is the fate of **democracy**, in whose eyes not all means are permitted, and to whom not all the methods used by her enemies are open *The Public Committee Against Torture in Israel*, cited in Weisberg 2008, pp. 181–182.

Each of these uses of the word "democracy" goes beyond its core meaning and adjusts (expands, modifies) that meaning in light of a particular context, which in all these cases included different theories of society and government.

Without more knowledge of the context to go on, it can be hard to see in (1a) what is inconsistent about democracy (i.e., voting) and voting on economic restrictions (which is, of course, voting). It can be hard to see in (1b) why parks would be evidence of democracy and, too, why in (1c) it is the fate of democracy not to torture people (when, in fact, the United States is, by some people's meanings, both a democracy and has tortured people).

Readers can only understand the situational meaning of "democracy" in (1a) if they have read Milton Friedman's work (an American economist who won the Nobel Prize in Economics in 1976), and related work, and know about neoliberal economic theories. This is the context to which the word "democracy" is being adapted in (1a). In this case, the job of the discourse analyst would be to show what "democracy" means in this context, why it means that, and how this has affected society and the world. The same sort of thing can be said for (1b) and (1c).

2.11 How core meaning is represented in the head

Psychologists, philosophers, and linguists have offered several different views of how the core meanings of words are represented in the human mind/brain (Elman 2004; Johnson-Laird 1983, 2006; Rorty 1961; Rosch 1975; Wierzbicka 1992; Wittgenstein 1953). I am going to develop only one such approach here.

The word "tree" is a sign or symbol for trees. But how do we know exactly what counts as a tree and what doesn't? The symbol itself surely doesn't tell us. The way we humans solve this problem is by treating certain sorts of trees as paradigm or typical examples of what a tree is. Then we treat "anything that is *sufficiently like* these exemplars" as worthy of having the word "tree" applied to it. On this view, the core meaning or semantic meaning of the word "tree" is "anything that sufficiently resembles exemplar trees".

Words take on various relationships to each other. For example, anything that sufficiently resembles the exemplars for "tree" also sufficiently resembles the exemplars for "plant" to count as a plant. Or, anything that sufficiently resembles the exemplars for "tree" does not sufficiently resemble the exemplars for "animal" to be counted as an animal. Words create a "system", a map of things in the world, an "ontology", a world-view. They "cut the world up" in a certain way.

It is obvious that different cultures cut up the world in different ways. There are many ways in which the world can be cut up into bits and pieces and boundaries. When we argue over whether THIS THING is sufficiently like THAT THING to be the SAME THING (to have the same word applied to it) we are arguing over boundaries (cuts, waves), ontologies, world-views, ways of being in the world.

Semantics is part of language as system ("grammar"). People in their "mental lexicons", or in dictionaries, can seek to capture the exemplars through images, paradigmatic examples, a list of features, some type of definition, or any combination of these. Definition, images, features, and examples can only capture a more or less well-bounded range of possibilities; rarely can they capture necessary and sufficient conditions that apply with no fuzzy edges.

For example, as we mentioned earlier, while a definition such as "a bachelor is an unmarried male" seems definitive, the Pope is an unmarried male, but not often referred to as a "bachelor" (Fillmore 1975). For a word such as "game" there is no very tight definition to be had that covers everything we apply the word to. Here we have only typical (paradigmatic) examples that share different features with each other, but not all the same ones, in much the way the genetically related people in a family share various features, but do not necessarily all have any one set of features in common all together. Wittgenstein (1953) called such concepts (like "game") "family resemblance" concepts.

Situational meanings apply core meanings in use. These are the meanings people give to a word in situations, based on their core meanings and the specific demands and features of the situation (Barsalou 1999a, 1999b). As an example, think of a bowl-like, large, cup-sized container with no handle in which people are drinking coffee, with two hands, in a fancy coffee store (something I saw once in Berkeley, California). This is certainly not a typical example of a coffee cup, but is it sufficiently like the typical examples that I should extend the meaning of "coffee cup" to use it here in this specific situation?

Recommended reading

Jean Aitchison (2012). *Words in the Mind: An Introduction to the Mental Lexicon.* Fourth Edition. London: Wiley-Blackwell.

References

Agar, M. (1994). *Language Shock: Understanding the Culture of Conversation.* New York: William Marrow.

Barsalou, L. W. (1999a). Perceptual Symbol Systems. *Behavioral and Brain Sciences* 22.4: 577–609.

Barsalou, L. W. (1999b). Language Comprehension: Archival Memory or Preparation for Situated Action. *Discourse Processes* 28.1: 61–80.

Becker, G. S. & Posner, R. A. (2006). On Milton Friedman's Ideas. Retrieved 24 September 2009 from www.becker-posner-blog.com/2006/11/on-milton-friedmans-ideas--becker.html

Becker, M. (2014). *The Acquisition of Syntactic Structure: Animacy and Thematic Alignment.* Cambridge, MA: Cambridge University Press.

Bergen, B. K. (2012). *Louder than Words: The New Science of How the Mind Makes Meaning.* New York: Basic Books.

Berlin, B. & Kay, P. (1991). *Basic Color Terms: Their Universality and Evolution.* Berkeley, CA: University of California Press.

Brown, G. & Yule, G. (1983). *Discourse Analysis.* Cambridge: Cambridge University Press.

Brown, L. R. (2008). *Plan B 3.0: Mobilizing to Save Civilization.* Washington, DC: Earth Policy Institute.

Cummings, E. E. "[anyone lived in a pretty how town]" from *Complete Poems 1904–1962,* edited by George J. Firmage. Copyright 1926, 1954, 1991 by the Trustees for the E. E. Cummings Trust. Copyright © 1985 by George James Firmage. Liveright Publishing Corporation.

Elman, J. L. (2004). An Alternative View of the Mental Lexicon. *Trends in Cognitive Sciences* 8: 301–306.

Fillmore, C. J. (1975). An Alternative to Checklist Theories of Meaning. *Proceedings of the First Annual Meeting of the Berkeley Linguistics Society,* pp. 123–131.

Goldberg, A. A. (1995). *Constructions: A Construction Grammar Approach to Argument Structure.* Chicago, IL: University of Chicago Press.

Hoffman, T. & Trousdale, G. (2013). *The Oxford Handbook of Construction Grammar.* Oxford: Oxford University Press.

Johnson-Laird, P. N. (1983). *Mental Models: Towards a Cognitive Science of Language, Inference, and Consciousness.* Cambridge: Cambridge University Press.

Johnson-Laird, P. N. (2006). *How We Reason.* Oxford: Oxford University Press.

Lakoff, G. (1987). *Women, Fire and Dangerous Things: What Categories Reveal about the Mind.* Chicago, IL: University of Chicago Press.

Rorty, R. (1961). Pragmatism, Categories, and Language. *Philosophical Review* 70.2: 197–223.

Rosch, E. E. (1975). Cognitive Representation of Semantic Categories. *Journal of Experimental Psychology: General* 104: 192–233.

Tomasello, T. (2003). *Constructing a Language: A Usage-Based Theory of Language Acquisition.* Cambridge, MA: Harvard University Press.

Weisberg, J. (2008). *The Bush Tragedy.* New York: Random House.

Whorf, B. L. (1956). *Language, Thought, and Reality: Selected Writings of Benjamin Lee Whorf.* Cambridge, MA: MIT Press.

Wierzbicka, A. (1992). *Semantics, Culture, and Cognition.* Oxford: Oxford University Press.

Williams, P. J. (1991). *The Alchemy of Race and Rights: Diary of a Law Professor.* Cambridge, MA: Harvard University Press.

Wittgenstein, L. (1953). *Philosophical Investigations.* Oxford: Blackwell Publishing.

3

Clauses and sentences

3.1 Types of clauses

This chapter will discuss what makes clauses and sentences more or less complex. Different degrees of complexity are an important part of what makes for different varieties of language. The language used by academics and specialists of other sorts is often more complex than everyday language. This complexity can in some circumstances help people do their work—like a more specialized tool—but in other circumstances can be a way to avoid saying clearly and straightforwardly what we mean. As a result, complex forms of sentence structure are loved by some and hated by others. We will start by discussing the nature of clauses and sentences as a way to build up to measures of more or less complexity for language in use.

Clauses are made up of a subject/topic and a predicate/comment. Subjects and predicates are all about "aboutness". "Mary married John" and "John married Mary" seem to mean pretty much the same thing. One cannot be true without the other one being true as well. Yet, in use, they mean different things. One is about Mary (and comments that she married John) and the other is about John (and comments that he married Mary). English, and all other languages, is organized in terms of subjects (what we are talking about in a statement or asking about in a question) and predicates (what we are saying or asking about it).

A **subordinate clause** is a clause that is loosely juxtaposed (linked) to another clause and functions like an adjunct to it:

1a. When she visits us,   my daughter takes her son to the beach
    ----------------   ----------------------------------
    subordinate clause   **main clause**

1b. My daughter takes her son to the beach,   when she visits us

   ------------------------------------   ----------------

               main clause   **subordinate clause**

1c. My daughter,   when she visits us,   takes her son to the beach

   ------------   ----------------   ------------------------

      main–   **subordinate clause**   **–clause**

Note how in (1c) the subordinate clause interrupts the main clause.

One clause can be embedded inside another clause as an integral part of that clause, not just an adjunct. Such clauses are called **embedded clauses**:

2a. My daughter thought that she should take her son to the beach

                        ----

                              embedded clause
                   (direct object of "thought")

2b. That she should take her son to the beach was clear to my daughter

   ----

            embedded clause
    (subject of "was clear")

The word "that" is an introducer for embedded clauses. It is sometimes optional as in "My daughter thought that she should take her son to the beach" (with "that") versus "My daughter thought she should take her son to the beach" (without "that"). In (2b) "that" is not optional, but must be present.

In (2a) "My daughter thought that she should take her son to the beach" is all one clause, because it is a subject ("my daughter") plus a predicate/comment ("thought that she should take her to the beach"). "That she should take her son to the beach" is also a clause (an embedded clause), since it has its own subject ("she") and predicate ("should take her son to the beach").

Clauses (with special modifications) can be embedded inside noun phrases as well. These sorts of clauses are called relative clauses (in (3a) "the boy" is the head of the relative clause, in (3b) "the package" is the head):

3a. [The boy (who) you saw yesterday] is back again today

          ----

               relative clause

      ----

              noun phrase

3b. I left [the package (that) you asked for] in the kitchen

----

relative clause

----

noun phrase

Note that "who" in (3a) and "that" in (3b) are optional. However, they are obligatorily in cases like "The boy [who saw you yesterday] is back again today" and "I left the package [that had your name on it in the kitchen]". In these cases, "who" and "that" are standing in for the subjects of the embedded clauses and cannot be left out.

Note the similarity, by the way, between relative clauses and questions:

4a. The boy who you saw ...
4b. Who did you see? The boy
4a. The boy who saw you ...
4b. Who saw you? The boy

Sometimes the verb in an embedded clause has an infinitival form ("to + verb"):

5a. My daughter forced   (her son   *to go*   to the beach)

infinitive

----

embedded clause

5b. My daughter wanted   (her son   *to go*   to the beach)

infinitive

----

embedded clause

Infinitives are verb forms that do not specify "tense" (i.e., time as present, past, or future). In "Mary knows that John blames himself", "blames" is present tense. In "Mary knows that John blamed himself", "blamed" is past tense. English uses "will" to mark the future ("Mary knows that John will blame himself"), though "will" has a number of other meanings as well. In "Mary wanted John to blame himself", no tense (time present, past, or future) is specified for "blame" and the infinitival form of the verb is used ("to blame").

Subordinate clauses can also have infinitival forms of the verb:

6. In order for her *to visit* us, my daughter drives three hours
             infinitive
    `-------------------------`
    subordinate clause

Embedded clauses with infinitives can have a missing subject which is understood to be the same as a previous subject as in "My daughter wanted to go to the beach". "To go to the beach" here is an embedded clause. The embedded clause "to go to the beach" means "my daughter to go to the beach", that is, "my daughter" is the missing, but understood, subject of "to go to the beach". Sometimes subordinate clauses are missing subjects as well, as in "While visiting us last year, my daughter took her son to the beach" (which means that while my daughter was visiting us last year, she took her son to the beach).

We can now define what a **sentence** is. A sentence is any clause or chain of clauses that can count as a complete statement, order, or question. So "My daughter took her son to the beach", when not accompanied by any more material, is a sentence (and, of course, a clause). And, "My daughter takes her son to the beach, when she visits us" is a sentence composed of two clauses (a main clause and a subordinate clause). "Even though she is reluctant, my daughter takes her son to the beach, when she visits us" is all one sentence (composed of three clauses, the first and third of which are both subordinate to the middle clause).

We have seen that a clause contains a subject and a predicate. We have also defined subordinate clauses and embedded clauses. Now, finally, we can define what main clauses are. Any clause that is not an embedded clause or a subordinate clause is a **main clause**:

7a. My daughter took her son to the beach
    `----------------------------------`
        main clause (and sentence)

7b. Yesterday, my daughter took her son to the beach for a while
    `--------------------------------------------------------`
        main clause (and sentence)

7c. While she was visiting, my daughter took her son to the beach for a while
    `------------------` `------------------------------------------`
    subordinate clause   **main clause**
    `--------------------------------------------------------`
                    sentence

7d. Mary thought that John was nice
----
subordinate clause
----
main clause (and sentence)

7e. My daughter took her son to the beach and he had a great time there
-----------------------------------   ----------------------------
       main clause   **main clause**
----
sentence

Recommended reading

Rodney Huddleston (1984). *Introduction to the Grammar of English*. Cambridge: Cambridge University Press.

3.2 Hidden clauses

The verb is the heart and soul of the clause. It is the central element of the predicate. Every time we have a verb we have a clause. English has a number of ways to turn verbs into other categories of words so that verbs can "slip into" other clauses as nouns or adjectives and still communicate a clause-worth of information.

For example, English allows verbs to be turned into nouns in a variety of different ways, for example: **destroy** Rome → the **destruction** of Rome; **attend** to details → her **attention** to details; **love** money → the **love** of money; **plan** for my vacation → my **plan** for my vacation. Note the similarity between the clause in (1a) and the noun phrase in (1b):

1a. Rome **destroyed** (verb) Greece (clause)
1b. Rome's **destruction** (noun) of Greece … (noun phrase)

Note also:

2a. Greece was **destroyed** (verb = passive voice) by Rome (clause)
2b. The **destruction** (noun) of Greece by Rome … (noun phrase)

(2a) is in the **passive voice**. Even though (2b) is a noun phrase it too seems to be in the passive voice as well.

Linguists call words like "destruction" **nominalizations**, because they are nouns related to verbs, here "destroy" (Kornfilt & Whitman 2011). Such words form what we will call **hidden clauses**, because a phrase is actually carrying a clause-worth of information (i.e., states or implies that a subject and predicate is involved in the meaning). So (1a) and (2a) are overt clauses and (1b) and (2b) are hidden clauses (noun phrases containing a clause-worth of information, namely a subject and predicate worth of information).

The term **hidden clause** is not a term in traditional grammar. I use it because I want to stress that a noun phrase like "Rome's destruction of Greece" is "like" a clause in that it has a subject ("Rome") and a predicate ("destruction of Greece" = destroy Greece). A noun phrase like "the destruction of Greece" is like a clause with a missing subject (one that can be supplied in a prepositional phrase as in "the destruction of Greece by Rome" or inferred from context).

Hidden clauses exist in English so that a clause-worth of information (as in 1a) can be made into a noun phrase and then inserted into a larger clause. They are way of packing information more tightly into one clause:

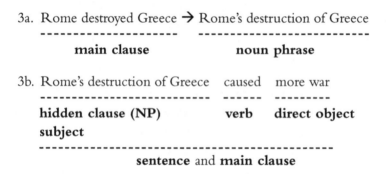

3a. Rome destroyed Greece → Rome's destruction of Greece
       ---------------------   ----------------------------
          main clause   **noun phrase**

3b. Rome's destruction of Greece   caused   more war
    --------------------------   ------   ---------
    hidden clause (NP)   **verb**   **direct object**
    subject
    ----
              sentence and **main clause**

Note that we could place the same information in (3b) into two sentences, rather than one:

3c. Rome destroyed Greece.   This caused more war.
    ---------------------   --------------------
    sentence and main clause   **sentence and main clause**

English also has ways to turn predicate adjectives (verb "to be" plus adjective) into hidden clauses as well, such as in the following examples:

4a. Mary was   clear   about her wishes
      helping   **adjective**
      verb   ------------------------
                adjective phrase

4b. Mary's clarity about her wishes   was important
------------------------------   -------------
hidden clause (noun phrase)   **predicate**
subject

5a. John is   loyal
     --   ----
    helping **adjective**
    verb

5b. John's loyalty   is without doubt
------------   --------------
hidden clause (noun phrase)   **predicate**
subject

Of course, hidden clauses do not have to be in subject position. They can appear anywhere any other noun phrase can appear:

6a. Mary's clarity about her wishes   impressed me
----
hidden clause (noun phrase)
subject

6b. I respected Mary's clarity about her wishes
                ----
                hidden clause (noun phrase)
                direct object

6c. I was impressed by Mary's clarity about her wishes
                ----
                hidden clause (noun phrase)
                object of preposition "by"

Some nominalized forms (nouns from verbs or adjectives) have become so common and routine in English that they have taken on quite different meanings than the verb or adjective from which they were derived. Thus, the verb "give" has a wider meaning than the noun "gift". The verb "report"

("Mary reported the crime") names something less formal than the noun "report" ("Mary's report on the crime"), which tends to mean a formal oral or written presentation. These routine nominalized forms tend to count not as a hidden clauses any longer, but just as a simple noun or noun phrase. In many other cases, however, the meanings of the verb or adjective and the nominalization derived from it are very similar. Some examples of this include: the verb "claim" ("Mary claimed that …) and the noun "claim" (Mary's claim that …); the predicate adjective "be clear" ("Mary was clear") and the noun "clarity" ("Mary's clarity …").

If you look up "nominalization" on the internet you will find a great many warnings not to use nominalizations in writing, that it creates "bad writing"; however, this is not true. Nominalizations are a mainstay of academic, scientific, and specialized forms of writing and are not uncommon in speech (Schleppegrell 2004). Like all grammatical forms, they are good when they serve a good purpose and bad when they serve no real purpose or when they serve a bad purpose like making things more obscure than they need to be,

There is yet another way that a clause-worth of information can be expressed in a phrase rather than a clause. In English, certain verb forms (e.g., the past participle) can be used as adjectives and, thus, function as the equivalent of a clause with a verb, without really being one:

7a. Someone abused children (clause)
        ------

        verb

7b. Abused children … (noun phrase)   are vulnerable
    ----

hidden clause
modifying verbal
adjective + noun

8a. The hackers stole the data
        ----

        verb

8b. The stolen data   circulate around the internet
    ----

hidden clause
modifying verbal
adjective + noun

Notice that in (7b) the phrase "abused children" raises the question "Who abused the children?" and in (8b) the phrase "stolen data" raises the question "Who stole the data?".

The final message here is that a hidden clause (Rome destroyed Greece → Rome's destruction of Greece; Mary is clear → Mary's clarity; Someone abuses children → abused children) allows a clause-worth of information (Rome destroyed Greece; Mary was clear; someone abused children) to be turned into a phrase so that this clause-worth of information can be inserted into a larger clause (Rome destroyed Greece → Rome's destruction of Greece changed history; Mary was clear → Mary's clarity is impressive; Someone abused children → Abused children need lots of help and support). We can take the non-traditional term "hidden clause" to mean "A phrase that contains a clause-worth of information, that is, that contains or implies material that could have been a subject and predicate in a real (verbal) clause".

3.3 A clause-worth of information

I want to define a measure that I will call "a clause-worth of information" (CWOI). I take this unit to be a basic unit of information in discourse. I want a measure that will tell us how many clauses' worth of information a speaker or a writer has communicated in a sentence or a given amount of time. A CWOI is the basic minimal unit of meaning beyond the word in speech (where idea units are often, but not always, a clause long) and writing.

Here is how the CWOI measurement works:

A. Any clause (embedded, subordinate, or main) constitutes one unit of CWOI.
B. Any hidden clause constitutes one unit of CWOI.

Thus, consider the cases below:

1a. My daughter took her son to the beach yesterday

----

main clause = 1 CWOI

Total CWOI = 1

1b. My daughter thinks   that her son is very smart
                     ----
                     embedded clause = 1 CWOI
----
           main clause = 1 CWOI
           Total CWOI = 2

1c. My daughter thinks   that her son wants   her to stay home
                                 ----
                                 embedded clause = 1 CWOI
                   ----
                   embedded clause = 1 CWOI
----
           main clause = 1 CWOI
           Total = 3 CWOI

1d. When she visits us,   my daughter takes her son to the beach
--------------------   ------------------------------------
subordinate Clause   **main clause**
= 1 CWOI   **= 1 CWOI**

           Total = 2 CWOI

1e. The historian believed   that Rome's destruction of Greece changed history
                       ----
                     hidden clause = 1 CWOI
                   ----
                   embedded clause = 1 CWOI
----
           main clause = 1 CWOI
           Total = 3 CWOI

1f. When it happened,   the destruction of Greece was believed to be catastrophic
-----------------   ---------------------   --------------
subordinate clause   hidden clause   **embedded**
                                          clause
= 1 CWOI   **= 1 CWOI**   **= 1 CWOI**
                   ----
                     main clause = 1 CWOI
                     Total = 4 CWOI

We can sketch out what (1f) means as below, where italicized words indicate material (subjects or other elements) that is missing and must be supplied by the listener or reader:

When it happened
the destruction of Greece = *something* destroyed Greece

was believed by *someone*
to be catastrophic

CWOI can be important when considering differences between speech and writing and between different genres of speech or writing. Academic lectures are speech, but will probably have a higher degree of CWOI per sentence than forms of more informal speech. Academic written prose tends to contain many sentences with quite high CWOI scores.

Another way to look at CWOI is as a measure of what we might call the **packaging of information** or **integration of information** in sentences. CWOI tells us how many clauses' worth of information are packaged or integrated into a given sentence. High CWOI scores mean a sentence has integrated a good deal of information together and will, thus, make heavy processing demands on listeners or readers.

For example, consider the sentence below (adapted—changed in form—from an academic journal article (Pollak, Vardi, Putzer Bechner, & Curtin 2005). I have **underlined each verb** and nominalized form:

2. The present paper <u>seeks</u> (verb)
to <u>clarify</u> (verb) and
and <u>extend</u> (verb)
previous <u>research</u> ("someone *researched* something)
<u>suggesting</u> (verb)
that physically <u>abused</u> children ("children were *abused* physically by someone")
<u>develop</u> (verb)
a strong <u>perceptual orientation</u> ("someone *orientates* to something perceptually")
to <u>threat</u> ("someone *threatens* someone")

The sentence in (2) has a CWOI score of nine. We can see what CWOI really amounts to and how complex it can be if we ask ourselves what questions a reader has to ask and answer in order to process and understand this sentence (Martin & Veel 1998). For each **underlined word** the listener or reader must ask what the subject and predicate is (and supply any missing material).

Recommended reading

Michael A. K. Halliday and James R. Martin (1993). *Writing Science: Literacy and Discursive Power*. London: Falmer.

3.4 Lexical density

Lexical density (Ure 1971) is another thing we can measure related to the complexity of processing information in communication. To see how this measure works we must first discuss different types of words. We will distinguish between three large classes of words: content words, function words, and proper nouns ("names").

Content words (sometimes also called "lexical words") belong to the major parts of speech: nouns, verbs, adjectives, and adverbs. These categories are said to be "open categories" in the sense that they each have a large number of different words in them and languages readily add new members to these categories through borrowing from other languages or the invention of new words.

Function words (also sometimes called "grammatical words") belong to smaller categories, categories that are said to be "closed categories" in the sense each category has relatively few members and languages are resistant to borrowing or inventing anew such words (though they sometimes do). Such categories as determiners (e.g., "the," "a/n," "this/that," "these/those"—these are also sometimes called "articles"); pronouns (e.g. "he/him," "she/her," "it," "himself," "herself"); prepositions (e.g., "in," "on," "to," "of"); and quantifiers (e.g., "some," "many," "all," "none") are function word categories.

Function words show how the content words in a phrase, clause, or sentence relate to each other, or how pieces of information fit into the overall ongoing communication. For example, the definite determiner "the" signals that the information following it is already "known" to the speaker and hearer. Pronouns signal that their referents have been previously mentioned, or are readily identifiable in the context of communication or on the basis of the speaker and hearer's mutual knowledge. Prepositions link nouns and noun phrases to other words (e.g., in "lots of luck," "of" links luck to lots; in "ideas in my mind," "in" links my mind to ideas; and in "look at the girl," "at" links the girl to the verb "look").

Since function words carry less of the real content of the communication (their job being to signal the grammar of the sentence), we can say that they tend to be informationally less salient than content words. They carry less contentful information. While they are certainly helpful, they are often dispensable, as anyone who has written a telegram knows (if there is anyone left who has!), or, more recently, a text message.

Proper nouns are names like "John", "San Francisco", "Mt Rushmore", and "Charles Darwin". Such names do not give functional or structural information about the relationships among words as do function words. And they do not carry as much contentful information as do content words like "man", "woman", and "child".

Content words carry the major content information in a sentence. So, one measure of what we might call the **lexical density** of a sentence is the number of content words (not counting proper nouns) in the sentence. People studying lexical density sometimes measure only the number of content words in main clauses. To see the issues here, consider the example below. I have bolded all the content words:

1a. When they **attempt** to **control employees' private behavior** //
----
   subordinate clause: 5 content words

   companies face adverse reactions
   ----
   main clause: 4 content words

1b. **Companies** that **attempt** to **control** their **employees' private behavior**, **face adverse reactions**
----
   main clause: 9 content words

In processing the main clause in (1b), listeners or readers must recognize nine content words and find their meanings in their heads. In (1a), on the other hand, listeners or readers must first recognize five content words and find their meanings in their heads in the subordinate clause. Once these words are recognized and understood, they serve as background knowledge for processing the main clause which has only four content words. This breaks the processing effort up into two cycles (we process language clause by clause), the first of which then supports the second.

Furthermore, when speakers or writers use subordinate clauses usually they are assuming that the information in them has already been introduced or is shared background knowledge with their listeners or readers. It is usually the content words in a main clause that are new information. Thus, the number of content words per main clause is often used as a measure of how lexically dense a given example of speech or writing is and how demanding it is in terms of processing lexical items (words).

Besides the number of content words per main clause, the frequencies (commonness in use) of words also affects processing load and difficulty. More frequent words (such as "give", "call", "person", and "number") are quicker to find in one's mental lexicon and quicker and easier to process and understand (due to our having had much more practice). Less frequent words (such as "evolution", "organism", and "convergent") are slower to be found and slower and harder to process and understand. Very often when a clause has lots of content words some of these are less frequent or common words, thereby increasing the processing burden. Note how many frequent words the example from vernacular speech in (2a) below has and how many less frequent words the example from academic writing in (2b) has (example from Fang & Schleppegrell 2008, p. 27):

2a. We have a **person** from Woodson who's in the **History Department**
----
main clause = 3 content words

And she's **interested** in **doing** some **research** into **Black history**
----
main clause = 4 content words

And she would **like** to get **involved** with the **school**
----
main clause = 3 content words

And here's her **number**
----
main clause = 1 content word

Give her a **call**
----
main clause = 2 content words

Note: "get" in "get involved with" is functioning like a helping verb as in "be involved with"

2b. A **pattern** of **evolution** in which **distantly related organisms evolve similar traits** is **called convergent evolution**
----
main clause = 11 content words

A sentence like (2b) puts a major burden on the reader or listener. All these content words must be recognized, understood, and held in mind, all while a person engages in one cycle of processing (we process clause by clause). This burden can only be reduced if the reader or listener has brought to the task lots of good background knowledge, including lots of practice with the uncommon words being used. That is why such language is a form of "insiders' language". Such "insiders' language" can sometimes facilitate the work of a group of people who share a common job, but it can sometimes also work to exclude others and sometimes to evade wider scrutiny about what is being said or done (Schleppegrell 2004).

(2a) spreads many words over many clauses and uses a lot of high frequency words. It is much easier to process.

Recommended reading

M. A. K. Halliday (1985). *Written and Spoken Language*. Geelong, VIC, Australia: Deakin University.

3.5 Principles

How many clauses' worth of information we integrate into a sentence and how lexically dense we make our clauses and sentences are choices we make based on the grammar of our language (system) and the demands of particular situations we face when we put language to use (discourse).

These choices (along with choices about vocabulary) are an important part of what makes for different varieties or styles of language (what we have called different social languages) used in different situations for different purposes. Thus, compare the two sentences below:

1a. Hornworms vary a lot in how well they grow
1b. Hornworm growth (nominal clause = hornworms grow)exhibits a significant amount of variation (nominal clause = hornworms vary)

Choices about how many clauses' worth of information to put in a single sentence, lexical density, and vocabulary (e.g., Germanic versus Latinate; frequent words versus less frequent words) mark these two sentences as quite different social languages. (1a) is in the vernacular and (1b) is a type of academic language.

So, we what we have been talking about in this chapter are the **principle of CWOI** (clause-worth of information); the **principle of lexical density**; and the **principle of vocabulary choice**.

References

Fang, Z. & Schleppegrell, M. L. (2008). *Reading in Secondary Content Areas*. Ann Arbor, MI: University of Michigan Press.

Kornfilt, J. & Whitman, J. (2011). Afterword: Nominalizations in Syntactic Theory. In J. Kornfilt & J. Whitman, Eds, *Nominalizations in Syntactic Theory, Lingua*, Special Issue, pp. 1297–1313.

Martin, J. R. & Veel, R., Eds. (1998). *Reading Science: Critical and Functional Perspectives on the Discourses of Science*. London: Routledge.

Pollak, S. D., Vardi, S., Putzer Bechner, A. M., & Curtin, J. J. (2005). Physically Abused Children's Regulation of Attention in Response to Hostility. *Child Development* 76.5: 968–977.

Schleppegrell, M. J. (2004). *The Language of Schooling: A Functional Linguistics Perspective*. Mahwah, NJ: Lawrence Erlbaum Associates.

Ure, J. (1971). Lexical Density and Register Differentiation. In G. E. Perren & J. L. M. Trimm, Eds, *Applications of Linguistics: Selected Papers of the 2nd International Congress of Applied Linguists*. London: Cambridge University Press, pp. 443–452.

4

Choice and discourse analysis

4.1 Idea units and intonation

This chapter is devoted to how intonation—the way we voice what we say—and grammar set up choices for speakers to make. These choices, in turn, become the basis of how hearers interpret what speakers say and why they have said it.

Thanks to the way the human brain and vocal system is built, speech is produced in small spurts. Unless we pay close attention, we don't usually hear these little spurts, because our ear puts them together and gives us the illusion of speech being an unbroken and continuous stream. In English, these spurts are often, though not always, one clause long. These spurts have been called many different things: "tone units", "intonation units", "idea units", or "thought units". Here, I will use the term **idea units**.

In the example below, taken from a story told by a seven-year-old African-American child at "sharing time" in school (Gee 2015), each speech spurt is one clause long, except 2 and 5 where the child has detached parts of clauses to be spurts on their own (children's idea units tend to be shorter than adults'). Each spurt is one idea unit and each spurt contains one "idea" (and, we will see, each has one focus stress):

1. there was a hook
2. on the top of the stairway
3. an my father was pickin me up
4. an I got stuck on the hook
5. up there
6. an I hadn't had breakfast

7. he wouldn't take me down
8. until I finished all my breakfast
9. cause I didn't like oatmeal either

We can we make a distinction between two types of information in an idea unit. First, there is information that is relatively new and relatively unpredictable. I will call this **new information**. Second, there is information that is already known or predictable. I will call this **old information**.

What is new and old information in English is indicated by **stress**. Stress is a *psychological concept, not a physical one*. English speakers can (unconsciously) use and hear several different degrees of stress in an idea unit, but this is not physically marked in any uniform and consistent way. Stress is physically marked by a combination of increased loudness, increased length, and by changing the pitch of one's voice (raising or lowering the pitch, or gliding up or down in pitch) on a word's primary ("accented") syllable. Any one or two of these can be used to trade off for the others in a quite complicated way. In any case, we hear stress as making a word more salient or noticeable.

In turn, the different stress patterns in an idea unit set up its **intonation contour** (Bolinger 1985; Halliday & Greaves 2004). Imagine a context where Mary and Sue are neighbors. In the recent past they have had several conversations about the fact that Sue's daughter is having a hard time finding a job, though she has been looking hard to find one. One morning Mary runs into Sue and asks "Did your daughter find a job yet?" A normal reply to this question could be:

1a. Yes, she found a job as a secretary at the university.

For now, we will leave the word "yes" aside. Given the context, "secretary" and "university" constitute new information. The hearer does not already know about them.

Since "find" and "job" are in the question and have been part of previous conversations, they are old information to the hearer. So is "she", since it refers back to "your daughter" in the question. Since these are all pieces of old information, the speaker could just as well have said: "Yes, as a secretary at the university" and left them out. Function words like "a", "at", and "the" are usually highly predictable and so old information. Note, even if we said "she finally found job university" we could predict what the function words would have been.

Speakers must put more stress on new information than on old information. Furthermore, the speaker must pick one piece of new information to have what we will call **focus stress**, the most prominent level of stress in an **intonation contour**. Each intonation contour (idea unit) has but one focus stress. The focus stress helps us identify the information that is most salient in the idea unit in the sense of being foregrounded or the center of attention.

We will assign numbers to the stress levels of each piece of information in (1a), with "1" being highest and "3" being lowest. "1" is for the focus stress. "2" is for new information that is not the focus. "3" is for old information that is a content word (not a function word). We will leave function words with no number, since they have minimal stress, just enough to be heard:

```
              3    3    2              1
1b.  Yes, she found a job as a secretary at the university
             ------ ---  --------      ---------
              Old   Old    New          Focus
```

(1b) is uttered as one intonation sequence or intonation contour with its focus at the end. In English, the focus is typically on the last content word in the unit, as it is here. When it is at the end, the usual interpretation is that the center of attention—the information being focused on or foregrounded— is all the new information in the idea unit—here: secretary and university. It is also possible in an utterance like (1b), that the speaker intends only the word with focus stress ("university") to be the center of attention—we can only tell whether this is the case from context or if the speaker puts extra stress (emphasis) on the word.

Sometimes, the focus stress is not at the end of the idea unit, as below:

```
               3    3    1                  2
1c.  Yes, she's found a job as a secretary at the university
              ------ ---  --------          ---------
               Old   Old    Focus             New
```

Here the speaker has chosen not to place the focus at the end, but on "secretary". Thus, the speaker has deviated from the norm (the focus on the last content word) and this takes on a special meaning: only "secretary" is taken as the center of attention or foregrounded information. The other new information is now rendered less salient (less foregrounded than "secretary") and the old information is least salient (because it can already be assumed to be known). One would utter (1c) instead of (1b) if the fact that the daughter being a secretary is taken as particularly salient or remarkable by the speaker (imagine, for example, the speaker saying something like "Yes, my PhD daughter found a job as a *secretary* at the university, can you believe it?").

Here is yet another way to answer the question:

```
        1     3     3     2              1
1d. Yes, she's finally found a job / as a secretary at the university
        ------------ ------  ---   --------    ---------
        Focus  Old   Old         New          Focus
```

Here we have two separate intonation contours. In the first "finally" is the focus and the only new information. Since it is not final (and there is no other new information anyway), it alone is taken as the most salient piece of information. In the second intonation sequence, the focus is at the end on "university" (the normal case), so both "secretary" and "university" are usually being taken as equally salient.

Let us return to the little word "yes". This word could have its own intonation sequence all by itself (a firm yes answer with a pause after it) or be treated as new information in another intonation sequence with the focus elsewhere:

```
      1         3     3     2              1
1e. Yes / she found a job as a secretary at the university
      ---       ------  ---   --------    ---------
      Focus     Old   Old     New         Focus

      2         3     3     2              1
1f. Yes she found a job as a secretary at the university
      ---       ------  ---   --------    ---------
      New       Old   Old     New         Focus
```

Finally, there is something called **emphatic stress.** Emphatic stress is extra strong and is intended to emphasize something and often to contrast it with something else. In the right context even function words can have emphatic stress:

2a. It's **MARY** I love, not Sue
2b. He threw the ball **AT** John, not to him
2c. I **DID** attend, but you didn't
2d. I told you to turn **RIGHT**, not left
2e. I said he went **TO** the house, not **IN** it

We have discussed here only the use of intonation (stress as marked by pitch changes, loudness, and lengthening) to demarcate idea units (also called "tone units" or "intonation units"). Intonation is also used for other purposes as well, such as to express attitude or emotion and to differentiate declarative sentences (with a fall in pitch at the end) from yes/no questions (with a rise in pitch at the end).

In English, individual words, no matter whether being said alone or with other words, carry more stress on their "accented syllable" than on the other syllables in the word and this can sometimes differentiate words from each other as in CON-test (noun: "enter the contest") versus con-TEST (verb: "contest the claim") and RE-bel (noun: "she's a real rebel") versus re-BEL (verb: "she rebelled early in life").

Recommended reading

David Brazil, Malcolm Coulthard, and Catherine Jones (1987). *Discourse, Intonation, and Language Teaching.* London: Longman. [A not widely known but excellent introduction to intonation.]

Wallace Chafe (1994). *Discourse, Consciousness, and Time: The Flow and Displacement of Conscious Experience in Speaking and Writing.* Chicago, IL: University of Chicago Press. [Best book to read to follow up on the ideas in this chapter.]

4.2 Choices

As we have discussed earlier, when we use language an important **principle of choice** operates. This principle says: What we say gets a good deal of its meaning from both what we said and what we didn't. How speakers produce idea units and where they place the focus stress in them are both choices that can be made in different ways. These choices signal what speakers want their hearers to take as new and old information and what information they want them to see as more or less salient in terms of what is being focused on, foregrounded, or is meant to be the center of attention. Speakers make these choices as they produce language in real time. These choices are accompanied by a host of other choices speakers make based on grammar. Choice is the heart and soul of communicating with language.

In writing, the idea unit is, of course, not based on stress and intonation units (there are none in writing) but on clauses. Clauses usually (but not always) express the basic idea units in writing. However, there is ample evidence that readers silently pronounce written words in their heads as they read (i.e., activate the phonological parts of their brain) and, in this sense, readers add back in the intonational contours. Good writers try to guide this process so that they retain some control over the meaning of what they have written (Dehaene 2009; Shaywitz 2005).

To start discussing the role of grammatical choices in interpretation, consider the example below, adapted from a news report (we will see the real version later below):

1. A white nationalist was bloodied Saturday (clause)
    while confronting protestors at a rally for Donald Trump (clause)

Since we are now talking about a written text, I will use the terms "writer" and "reader", but what I say applies, as well, to speakers and listeners. Readers of the text above can ask themselves why the author chose the word "bloodied" rather than a list of other possibilities, such as "injured", "hurt", or "wounded". From an accompanying picture the news source ran, the man looked like he had received a cut to his forehead that was bleeding, though it did not seem to be a very serious injury. So why not say that he got a cut on his forehead?

Readers who are familiar with the conventions of news reporting know that news stories are supposed to draw readers' attention from the first line on and often use blood, violence, or conflict to do so, things humans are prone to pay avid attention to. But the choice of "bloodied" also takes a perspective on this event that sees the man's injury as almost a part of war, an assault from an angry "mob", rather than an accident stemming from close physical contact and jostling.

What this short discussion of choice shows is that interpretation comes in part both from what other words (or other sorts of choices) the reader knows (or thinks) were available to the writer (but were not chosen) and also what the reader knows about the social conventions of a particular practice (e.g., news reporting) and its concomitant variety of language (social language). One can see here that communication between people who do not share a good deal of linguistic, social, and cultural knowledge is liable to be very vexed.

For "bloodied" to be meaningful (and to do its work as news reporting) in (1), readers must (at least) unconsciously know that it was chosen instead of other possibilities like "injured", "damaged", "hurt", "cut", and so forth, and that this choice matters and indicates a certain intended meaning and effect. This principle of choice and meaning applies widely in society. If I show up at a formal event in jeans, this means something and has certain effects because you know I chose jeans instead of, say, a suit.

Recommended reading

Ferdinand de Saussure (1986). *Course in General Linguistics*. Chicago, IL: Open Court. Originally published in French in 1916.

4.3 Choices: Topic-comment

We are now going to discuss some other sorts of consequential choices speakers make. Consider (1) again:

1. A white nationalist (**subject/topic**)
    was bloodied Saturday while confronting protestors at a rally for Donald Trump (**predicate/comment**)

English clauses take the form of a subject and a predicate. The subject is the **topic** of the clause; it is what the clause is about. The predicate is what is being said or asked about the subject, which we can call the **comment**. In (1) the subject/topic is "a white nationalist". The predicate/comment (what the speaker/writer wants to say about the topic) is "was bloodied Saturday while confronting protesters at a rally for Donald Trump".

Now consider a different choice of topic and comment:

2. Protestors (**subject/topic**)
    bloodied a white nationalist while he was confronting them at a rally for Donald Trump (**predicate/comment**)

Readers have to ask why the writer has chosen to talk about the white nationalist (topic) and tell us what happened to him (comment) as in (1) and not instead talk about the protestors (topic) and what they did (comment). In reality, both things happened. (1) surely implies (2): that the protestors, intentionally or not, injured the white nationalist. Nonetheless, the writer must choose one or the other (or yet other perspectives that could have been taken).

4.4 Choices: Agents

Subjects often (but not always) name an **agent** (actor) in an action. There are ways, however, in English to not mention an agent even when one is present. For example, a writer could say either "Protestors (agent) bloodied a white nationalist" or "A white nationalist was bloodied" (a passive voice form) where the writer has not mentioned the agent (either because the writer does not know who did it or does not want to say). Of course, the writer could also say "A white nationalist was bloodied by protestors". So, consider three possible choices:

1. A white nationalist was bloodied [**by an unnamed agent**] Saturday while confronting protesters at a rally for Donald Trump.
2. A white nationalist was bloodied by protestors [**agent**] Saturday while confronting them at a rally for Donald Trump.
3. Protesters [**agent**] at a rally for Donald Trump bloodied a white nationalist Saturday when he confronted them.

Why did the writer write version (1) and not either (2) or (3) (or some other version)? The reason the writer used the version she did may be that she wants to leave it open whether the injury was an "accident" or "on purpose" (either way, the protestors were intentional or accidental agents). Stating the agent overtly as in (2) and (3) invites the implication that the event was intentional, though it does not actually say so (an utterance like "Mary injured John" implies, but does not directly assert, purposefulness, but that implication can be mitigated as in "Mary injured John when her loving hug sadly triggered his bad back to spasm"). Note, too, that putting "protestors" in subject position, as in (3), gives them a more central role and implies purposefulness more than the passive voice version in (2) does.

4.5 Choices: Asserted-assumed

Consider our adapted news report again:

1. A white nationalist was bloodied Saturday while confronting protestors at a rally for Donald Trump

In (1) the clause "while confronting protestors at a rally for Donald Trump" is a subordinate clause. It is adjoined to the main clause "A white nationalist was bloodied Saturday". Main clauses state **foregrounded** and **asserted** information. Subordinate clauses state information that is **backgrounded** and **assumed** (taken-for-granted).

The grammatical choice as to what information to assert and what to assume sets up a social contract between the writer and reader. The reader is supposed to address any comments or disagreements to the asserted information and simply take the assumed information for granted. So, in the case of (1), the reader is supposed to agree or disagree with "A white nationalist was bloodied Saturday" and take "while confronting protestors at a rally for Donald Trump" for granted. So, while a reader might ask, "How badly was he really hurt?" or "Was it an accident or done on purpose?", the reader is not supposed to ask things like "Was it really a confrontation?" or "Was this really a rally for Trump?".

Of course, listeners and readers do not have to be compliant and obey this social contract. However, if they do not, they risk alienating, irritating, or angering the speaker or ignoring the intentions of the writer. And, of course, speakers and writers can seek to use this social contract to manipulate listeners and readers into not bringing up (or not thinking too much about) what they don't want brought up or thought about. Consider (2) below in this regard:

2. Yesterday, protestors shouted down Donald Trump when he was telling the simple truth about immigration in this country.

Here the writer does not want us to dispute the claim that Trump was telling the simple truth, so he makes this information not the asserted information (the claim he is actually making), but backgrounded, assumed, taken-for-granted information. It would be "rude" to respond with "Was it really the truth, I doubt it?". Such a reader would not be a compliant reader. In this case, readers who support Trump are more likely to be compliant. This shows that choices like this can be made, not just to manipulate, but to bond, so to speak, with the readers, by assuming the reader is "like us" and agrees with us, and so we can assume that we share certain taken-for-granted viewpoints.

Note

In questions, the main clause is not asserted, but expresses the information we are questioning. Subordinate clauses are assumed information and not the focus of questioning. So, in "Did Bill get hurt while attending the Trump rally?", the speaker is questioning whether Bill got hurt and assuming the listener will agree or take for granted that Bill was attending the Trump rally. So, too, a question like "Why was Trump shouted down when he was telling the simple truth about immigration in this country" would be manipulative, ironic, or bonding in different contexts given that the "telling the simple truth" clause is assumed information and yet would be contentious to some people and not to others.

4.6 How we make and interpret choices

We have been using an adapted (simplified) version of what an actual reporter wrote. Here is the real version:

1. A member of a white nationalist group was bloodied Saturday while confronting a large group of protesters outside the site of a Washington conference celebrating Donald Trump's presidential victory
    http://www.cnn.com/2016/11/19/politics/donald-trump-protest/

As discourse analysts, we usually assume in a case like this that both the writer and her readers know English and know the social language and social conventions used for news reporting. The writer (Laurie Ure, a CNN producer) drew on both her linguistic knowledge and her knowledge of the conventions of news reporting—consciously and unconsciously—to make choices about how to write what she wrote. Readers must draw on their linguistic knowledge and knowledge about news reporting to ask themselves why she wrote the sentence the way she did and not in the many other possible ways she could have.

Another thing we usually assume is that the writer and reader both share social knowledge, here knowledge about things like white nationalism, Donald Trump, and his pursuit of and election to the presidency of the United States. Note that the writer does not even mention what the protestors are protesting (i.e., Trump and what they take to be his racist views and those of some of his supporters), because she takes this to be something her readers will already know.

Readers must ask themselves (consciously or unconsciously): "What perspective on reality is this writer trying to express linguistically"? That is, readers must construct in their heads a particular model of—or perspective on—reality (here, on the event being reported) based on how the writer has written what she has written.

Readers will realize—thanks to their tacit linguistic knowledge as speakers of English and consumers of news—that other options were available to the reporter. Readers who know more about the actual event will be aware of even more options. Here are just two of them:

2. A white nationalist was bloodied Saturday while provoking protestors at an annual Washington white-nationalist conference which this year was celebrating Donald Trump's election
3. A large group of protestors bloodied a man attending the annual Washington National Policy Institute conference, which this year was celebrating the election of Donald Trump, when he approached them with a video camera and a microphone in what appeared to be an attempt to film an interview with one of the protestors.

All three of these versions are possible perspectives to take on the event. Some require knowing more about the event than others do, but the reporter knew a good deal about the event. All these perspectives are (or certainly can be) true. While the reporter might be lying or wrong, the real issue here is that even if all three are true, we are dealing with different perspectives on reality. We can and must sometimes discuss which perspective is "better" (and the criteria for this remain to be explicated), but truth or accuracy does not settle the matter alone. This point about grammar as a perspective-taking device is not a political point; it is an empirical point about how language works.

Recommended reading

William F. Hanks (1995). *Language and Communicative Practices*. New York: Westview.

4.7 Strangers

In the last section I said that we discourse analysts usually assume speakers/ writers and listeners/readers know the language being used and share a good deal of knowledge. But this need not be the case. We can also study how people who fail to share some important aspects of knowledge communicate and how interpretation works in these cases. Often, people who are "strangers" in the sense that they do not share a good deal of linguistic, social, and cultural knowledge can teach us to pay attention to things that are normally so routine and taken-for-granted for us that we do not think about them and reflect on them in any very conscious or explicit way (Halliday & Matthiessen 1999; van Dijk 1997a, 1997b). Sometimes, we can be jolted into recognition by novel understandings or questions from people who don't share our routine and taken-for-granted knowledge.

One very useful strategy for discourse analysts is to try to make the linguistic, social, and cultural assumptions we take for granted **strange** (Shklovsky 1965). This means that we try to see these assumptions in an overt way and from perspectives that can make them seem strange and worth thinking about anew. We can call this the **making strange technique** (and one good way to engage in this technique is to study people navigating ways with words and social and cultural practices to which we, but not them, are insiders or vice-versa, to have outsiders study us as insiders).

Of course, all of us are insiders in some contexts and outsiders in others. When I first moved from working in linguistics departments to working in Schools of Education, I had never been in an American public school in my life. So, when I first went into schools, I was an outsider and saw as strange what my educational colleagues who had visited and worked in many a school took for granted.

Here is one example of something that seemed very strange to me, though it did not seem strange to my colleagues. When I was visiting a school early in my time in education, I saw a teacher working with a small group of fourth-grade students. She first dictated a sentence to them that the students were to write down. The sentence was "I love the puppy". Then she dictated a list of words, one at a time, which the children were to write down with correct spelling. After they had finished, the teacher asked the children how the word "love" in the original sentence is spelled and how each word on the list (one after the other) is spelled. The children were supposed to correct each spelling, if they had made a mistake, only after the teacher had elicited the correct spelling orally from the children.

Below is what one girl, who happened to be African-American, wrote on her list. Note that "sume" ("some") and "shuve" ("shove") are spelled incorrectly:

___dove_____
___sume____
___glove____
___one_____
___shuve____
___come____
___none_____

As I mentioned, the teacher had the children correct the original sentence and then each word in the list one-by-one, eliciting the correct spelling of each item from the group as a whole. When she got to "some", the second word on the list, the girl corrected it, then noticed what the spelling pattern was and went ahead and corrected "shuve" further down the list. The teacher stopped her and reprimanded her, saying that they had to go "one at a time" and she shouldn't "go ahead".

The teacher moved on to have the small group of children engage in a "picture walk" of a book. This is an activity where children "read the pictures" in a book, using each picture in turn to predict what the text in the book will say. The girl bounced in her chair repeatedly, enthusiastically volunteering for each picture. The teacher told her to calm down. The girl said, "I'm sorry, but I'm SO happy". The teacher responded: "Well, just calm down".

It seemed strange to me that even though the girl's moving forward to correct her errors showed that she had caught on to the spelling pattern being taught, and wanted to correct all her errors accordingly, she was reprimanded. I would have thought that the teacher would have said, "Hey, great, you got it". I was also surprised by the teacher's response to the girl saying "I'm sorry, but I'm SO happy". In everyday life if someone says "I'm SO happy", the polite thing to do is to ask them why. This teacher was well respected in the school and neither she nor the children appeared to see anything odd going on.

The girl happened to be African-American, though I had no idea at that point whether race played any role in this at all. What I did later come to realize was that the teacher was as focused, or maybe even more focused, on teaching students to follow guidelines and remain well-ordered than on the content of the lesson alone (Bernstein 2000).

I also, after much more collection of data, came to see that many of the teachers in this school operated with a taken-for-granted principle, something like this: With young children, if "you give them an inch, they'll take a mile". They believed that if you let children get away with small things, the children would quickly escalate to lots of noise and disruption. This was not something I personally knew anything about and was, thus, not anything I saw as a normal assumption.

The point here is not that I was right and the teacher was wrong (Cazden 2001). The point is that I saw all this as strange since I was such a stranger to these practices. At the same time, however, teachers, like all of us, sometimes need to rethink what they routinely do and assume and reflect on these things at a conscious level. Routines help us function efficiently, but they can sometimes become dysfunctional or even do harm. Perhaps, for example, responding to the girl's happiness could have helped build her emotional affiliation with the lesson, the teacher, and schooling. In any case, the making strange technique is a useful way to begin asking why what we take for granted came to be so taken and whether we should reconsider this "taken-for-granted-ness" or not.

By the way, what I have said thus far does not tell us whether the fact that the girl is African-American is relevant or not. We face here a controversy in discourse analysis. Some discourse analysts believe that things like race, class, and gender are relevant only when in a social interaction they are directly or indirectly referenced in some way. Others believe that there are social categories in a society that are so important (or historically vexed) that they are always relevant whether alluded to in some fashion or not.

In the schools I was visiting at the time of the events described above, teachers often turned the lights out when children made noise, in order to get them to be quiet. I came to notice that it was very often one of the more ebullient kids in the class that caused the lights to go out. This makes sense. The teacher, thanks to the "give them an inch, they'll take a mile" principle, is going to turn the lights off at the first sign of noise and, thus, the more ebullient children are likely to be the first to go over the line, however minor their noise making may have been.

People from different cultural groups have different normal degrees of what we might call "pitch". Some groups tend to show emotion and involvement more strongly—to be more "lively"—than other groups. In these schools, which were in Wisconsin, the white children and teachers tended to be lower pitched than the African-American children, indeed, they were lower pitched than white people in some other cultural groups (Kochman 1981). So, in these schools, some of the African-American children were a step ahead of the other children and went over the low-bar noise line just before other children were about to cross it. Thus, they "caused" the lights to go out more commonly, but not because they were particularly noisy or disruptive (indeed, the little girl we just discussed was quite enthusiastic about her academics), but because they were a bit higher pitched than many of the white children.

By the way, there is nothing inherently good or bad about a groups' pitch level (and not all members of a group behave the same). At the same time, there are some groups (defined by culture or class) whose pitch level is low enough that they can seem to others "disinterested". And there are some groups whose pitch level is high enough that they can seem to others "excited". There is a continuum here, not a binary distinction, but when the poles interact, interesting things—some of them unfortunate—can happen. Pitch level can vary even within groups that share aspects of a larger culture (e.g., Jewish people from a Western European background tend to be lower pitched than Jewish people from an Eastern European background, and people from some areas in Italy tend to be higher pitched than most white people from England, see Tannen 1984).

When the teachers turn out the lights, they have long since ceased to reflect much on the matter and the assumptions behind it. It is just routine practice. So, it is easy to see the child—and whatever is salient about the child—to be the "trouble", not the practice and the assumptions behind the act of turning off the lights to gain quiet. If one realized that noise can be a sign of disruption or of learning—and we need to know which is which—the practice might well change. If one realized that people have different normal degrees of "pitch", the bar for lights-out might be raised.

Recommended reading

Alessandro Duranti (1992). *Linguistic Anthropology*. Cambridge: Cambridge University Press.

References

Bernstein, B. (2000). *Pedagogy, Symbolic Control, and Identity: Theory, Research, Critique*. Revised Edition. Lanham, MD: Rowman & Littlefield.

Bolinger, D. (1985). *Intonation and Its Parts: Melody in Spoken English*. Stanford, CA: Stanford University Press. (Bolinger was the master of intonation.)

Cazden, C. (2001). *Classroom Discourse: The Language of Teaching and Learning*. Second Edition. Portsmouth, NH: Heinemann.

Dehaene, S. (2009). *Reading in the Brain: The Science and Evolution of a Human Invention*. New York: Viking Adult.

Gee, J. P. (2015). *Social Linguistics and Literacies: Ideology in Discourses*. Fifth Edition. London: Routledge.

Halliday, M. A. K. & Greaves, W. S. (2004). *Intonation in the Grammar of English*. London: Equinox.

Halliday, M. A. K. & Matthiessen, C. M. I. M. (1999). *Construing Experience Through Meaning: A Language-Based Approach to Cognition*. New York: Continuum.

Kochman, T. (1981). *Black and White Styles in Conflict*. Chicago, IL: University of Chicago Press.

Shaywitz, S. (2005). *Overcoming Dyslexia: A New and Complete Science-Based Program for Reading Problems at Any Level*. New York: Vintage.

Shklovsky, V. (1965). Art as Technique. In L. T. Lemon & M. J. Reis, Eds., *Russian Formalist Criticism: Four Essays*. Omaha, NE: University of Nebraska Press, pp. 3–24.

Tannen, D. (1984). *Conversational Style: Analyzing Talk Among Friends*. New Edition 2005. Oxford: Oxford University Press.

van Dijk, T. A., Ed. (1997a). *Discourse as Structure and Process*. London: Sage.

van Dijk, T. A., Ed. (1997b). *Discourse as Social Interaction*. London: Sage.

5

Identities and discourses

5.1 Identities: Activity-based identities

There is a difference between an action and activity. When a pitcher in a baseball game throws the ball towards home plate from the pitcher's mound, that is an action. But pitching is also an activity that is done in similar (but not identical) ways repeatedly and is regulated (in terms of how it is done) by groups and institutions, namely, baseball leagues and the sport of baseball. In work on social and cultural issues, the term "practice" is often used instead of "activity".

Activities in the world are organized around a certain "identity" (Hacking 2006; Mishler 2000). Consider, as an example, "birding". Certain people are what we might call "real birders". By this I mean that they are "into" birding, identify themselves as birders, are adept at birding, and are recognized by other adept birders as a birder.

I have used birding as an example of an **activity-based identity** (practice-based identity). Of course, any society is just chock full of such identities. Consider, for example, the very partial list below:

Mime
Policeman
Gamer
Kindergarten teacher
Social activist
Linguist

Physicist
Gang member
Doctor
Birder
Fan-fiction writer
Craft-furniture maker
Carpenter

Activity-based identities are named by both a noun (for BEING) and a verb (for DOING). So, birders bird, gardeners garden, gamers game, and physicists do physics. However, for any activity-based identity, these general names (e.g., gardeners, gardening) hide the large amount of diversity that the activity-based identity encompasses. There are many different types of gardeners, for instance, and there are different ways to distinguish among different types of gardeners.

Gardeners can grow one type of plant or many; they can be fruit and vegetable gardeners or flower gardeners or both; they can do organic gardening or not; they can garden to landscape or eat; they can engage in community gardening or garden at home; they can be casual gardeners, high-tech gardeners, large-scale gardeners, or serious gardeners with small plots; they can be container gardeners, raised-bed gardeners, urban gardeners, indoor gardeners, or even butterfly gardeners (planting plants that will attract butterflies). These are only a few of the many different things gardeners can be.

Activity-based identities are identities that people adopt by free choice. It is important to note, though, that activity-based identities are not IN a person. They are a reciprocal relationship between a person and a social group and its core defining activities. Such identities change in history as groups change their activities, norms, values, or standards. Some activity-based identities go out of existence and new ones arise. Activity-based identities are ways for people to identify with something outside of themselves, something that other people do and are.

Recommended reading

Ian Hacking (1986). Making Up People. In T. C. Heller, M. Sosna, and D. E. Wellbery, with A. I. Davidson, A. Swidler, and I. Watt, Eds., *Reconstructing Individualism: Autonomy, Individuality, and the Self in Western Thought*. Stanford, CA: Stanford University Press, pp. 222–236.

5.2 Identities: Relational identities

There is another sort of identity, besides activity-based identities, what we will call **relational identities** (Appiah 2005; Taylor 1989; Taylor, Appiah, Habermas, Rockefeller, Walzer, Wolf & Gutmann 1994). Relational identities are defined in terms of relations, contrasts, or oppositions between different types of people. Here is a non-exhaustive list:

IDENTITIES	EXAMPLES
Cultural	Native-American, Latino
Ascribed	ADHD, gifted
Gender	woman, trans-man
Sexuality	heterosexual, gay
Attributes	cancer survivor, blind
Ideological	conservative, libertarian
Religious	Christian, Hindu
Class	working class, 1%
Family	the Smith family, the Billings lineage
Age	teen, elderly

Relational identities are often imposed on or assigned to people, the result of "fate", or picked up in early socialization in life within families. Even political viewpoints such as being liberal or conservative are strongly connected to our families and upbringing.

Relational identities are defined in relation to, often in contrast or opposition to, other identities. Teens are defined in relation to and in contrast to other age groups. Native-Americans are defined in relation to and in contrast to other ethnic groups. People with ADHD are defined in relation to and in contrast to other disabilities and abilities. When humans start classifying by oppositions and contrasts, distinctions all too often become invidious, caught up with "better" and "worse" sorts of judgments.

Relational identities change or disappear if the other identities they are contrasted with change or disappear. If humans died by 20 or so, there would be no need for a teen category (teens then would just be adults) and the category of elderly would change quite a bit. If all non-African-American people in the United States disappeared tomorrow, then African-Americans would cease to be African-Americans and would become just "Americans". Conservatives in the United States have moved so far to the right over the last few decades that politicians once called conservative would now be viewed as moderates (e.g., President Dwight Eisenhower).

Each of these sorts of relational identities can exist in three separate ways: (1) a classificatory label that other people apply to you, but which you reject or don't much care about; (2) a label that you own and identify with; and (3) a label you are conflicted about.

When people choose to own and identify with a relational identity, for them, then, it is not just a classification that was imposed on them or which they inherited. It is how they see themselves. For example, some deaf people see deafness not just as a bodily attribute, but as a valuable and distinctive culture with its own language (American Sign Language) and ways of being, doing, and knowing. They refer to themselves as "Deaf" with a capital "D" and, in this way, they turn a classification ("deaf") into an identity they highly value and accept. Being Big D Deaf is defined not by how much hearing you do or do not have, but by values, norms, and activities in which people engage together (Padden & Humphries 2005).

A relational identity can, thus, become much like an activity-based identity. Being Big "D" Deaf is an example. People can even freely identify with relational identities like "manic-depressive" or "cancer survivor" (Martin 2007). They see such an identity not just as a label someone else has given them, but as a way of being in the world connected to special ways of doing and knowing. They sometimes even join with others to celebrate the identity and redefine it in positive terms. This is one way they seek to own the identity rather than be trapped in it.

Recommended reading

James Paul Gee (2017). *Teaching, Learning, Literacy in Our High-Risk High-Tech World: A Framework for Becoming Human.* New York: Teachers College Press. [Parts of this section and the preceding one are based on this book.]

5.3 Discourses

I argued earlier that when we use language we always formulate perspectives (viewpoints) on reality, not "reality straight", so to speak. To see how this works, consider what happens when we see things in physical space. We always see things from some perspective, from some physical place where we are located at the time. If we look at a mountain from the east, it looks different than it does from the west, north, or south. It looks different from up above than it does from down below; it looks different from far away than it does from close up. It is one and the same mountain, but we cannot see it all at once as one thing. We must see it from a particular place. We have to stand some place and cannot stand every place at once.

The mountain example shows that a perspective on something (a view of it from some place) is a relationship between a viewer, a place where the viewer is located, and a thing we see, often only partially. Much the same thing is true of the perspectives we take on things when we use language.

When we formulate a perspective on something using language, where we are located helps determine our perspective (what we see) just as much as where we are standing helps determine how we see the mountain. But where are we located when we speak? What sort of spaces are we in? We are in what I will call **the social space of identities**.

When you speak, your listeners need to know "where you are coming from" and this is an identity of some sort that helps your listeners to know where in social space you are standing for this encounter. Let's say, as an example, a doctor named Mary wants to speak to a patient named Fred. Fred just so happens to be Mary's friend, but also himself a doctor. Mary could speak to Fred as a friend speaking to a friend (the friend-to-friend space); as a doctor speaking to a fellow doctor (the doctor-to-doctor space); or as a doctor speaking to her patient (the doctor-patient space).

What does a doctor need to have to speak as a doctor to someone as a patient? Well, a patient, of course, but also other things as well. She needs accepted norms of how to dress, talk, act, and interact. She needs certain sorts of places like an office or a hospital. She needs certain types of knowledge, beliefs, and values, or, at least, to be able to get the patient to think she has these. She needs certain sorts of certificates, which may well be on display. All these things, the doctor did not make, they came to her from the work of others and from the work of institutions now and in history.

When doctors seek to speak as a doctor to a patient as a patient, they usually speak not only as a doctor in general, but as a doctor of a certain kind. They may, for instance, speak as a modern humanist doctor (where the patient is a co-participant in his or her own care), as a family doctor, a specialist of a certain sort, or some other kind of doctor.

To speak as a doctor (of a certain kind), the doctor must get recognized by others as speaking as a doctor (and often a doctor of a certain kind). If she does not, she has failed to be in the doctor-patient space and is in some other part of social space. So, for example, imagine Mary says to Fred in her office, "You have lost too much weight, you need to eat more". Fred might understand this as a doctor talking to a patient (medical advice) or as a friend talking to a friend (or both). If Fred takes it as just a social remark from one friend to another, and Mary meant it as medical advice, Mary has failed to speak from the doctor-to-patient space and has been taken by Fred to be speaking from the friend-to-friend space. Of course, Mary could stand in both spaces at the same time and be heard as giving advice (both as a concerned friend and as a medical advisor based on a check-up).

When Mary seeks to speak to Fred as a doctor to a patient, she requires the existence of a doctor-to-patient social space (composed of accepted norms, values, ways of speaking, acting, and interacting, as well as offices, hospitals, medical practices, and so forth). When she seeks to speak as a doctor, she is seeking to speak and act out of a certain identity, the identity of a doctor or often a specific kind of doctor.

I will call an identity (e.g., doctor, gamer, African-American) and all the stuff it requires in order to be enacted a **Discourse**, with a capital D (Gee 2014, 2015). Discourses are ways of enacting and recognizing socially significant identities based on how a person uses all the "stuff" required to get recognized as having that identity. So, Mary must speak, interact, and act in certain ways; use tools and technologies in certain ways; display certain sorts of knowledge, beliefs, and values; and inhabit certain sorts of places in certain ways to get recognized as a doctor—and often a doctor of a certain type—speaking to a patient (and, yes, often a patient of a certain type—patients must "play the game" as well).

Smaller Discourses (e.g., types and sub-types of doctors or gardeners) exist inside bigger ones (e.g., doctors or gardeners). Discourses do not always—or even often—have sharp boundaries. For example, what counts, at a given place and time, as a doctor and as a "quack" has a "gray" area in between and shifts with time and place. And Discourses are always partly defined and function in terms of their relationships to other Discourses. For example, doctors are defined in part in terms of their relationships to nurses, therapists, lawyers, medical researchers, and so forth.

Mary can fail when she attempts to get recognized as a doctor speaking to a patient as a patient. Perhaps, when she speaking to Fred, he dismisses her medical advice as just social chat among two old friends. Perhaps, in another context, a patient or other doctors dismiss Mary as not a "real doctor" because they question her credentials, skills, values, or beliefs. In some medical contexts, osteopathic doctors are accepted as "real doctors", in other contexts they are not or not fully. So, too, for example, someone can be recognized as a "real Indian" (Native-American) by other "real Indians" in some contexts and not others (the term "real Indian" here is an emic term used by some Native-Americans and Native-American groups). Recognition is not once and for all and it does not necessarily work the same way in all situations or contexts.

Why do I use the word "Discourse" with a big "D"? In English, we capitalize proper nouns (names), but not common nouns (categories). So, when I first capitalized the word "Discourse" in my writings to mean the social spaces from which we speak and act, it was considered by copy-editors to be wrong, to be "bad English". However, I used the term because I wanted to stress the fact that when "Mary" (a person with a name we capitalize) speaks as a doctor (and not, say, as a feminist, friend, or avid gamer) the Discourse of doctors speaks as well. Mary cannot speak and act as a doctor (or a kind of doctor) without the Discourse and the Discourse cannot exist without people speaking and acting as part of it and on its behalf.

So, in history, as, say, doctors talk to nurses, or as police talk to gang members, the Discourse of doctors speaks to the Discourse of nurses and the Discourse of policemen speaks to the Discourse of gangs (and vice versa) and they shape and change each other through time. It is as if a Discourse—like being a doctor or a gang member—is a "big person" that uses the voices and bodies of us little people to engage in conversation with other Discourses. However, though Discourses are big and we are little, Discourses need us to speak and act for them and we can sometimes change them in the process, since they can only guide us, but cannot fully determine exactly what we say and do and how we say it and do it.

To sum up, then: There are no basketball players without the Discourse of basketball (players; ways of talking, acting, and interacting; rules; balls; courts; hoops; uniforms; and teams). A person cannot be recognized as playing basketball or being a basketball player without coordinating in the "right ways" with other people and rules, ways of talking, acting, and interacting, courts, balls, hoops, and appropriate clothes. And, the Discourse of basketball (how we enact and recognize basketball and basketball players) cannot exist without people, though different people keep it alive as an enterprise—as a Discourse—at different times and places. And, Discourses change as people innovate in certain ways (within bounds, of course, in basketball and in other Discourses).

Recommended reading

D. Lawrence Wieder and Steven Pratt (1990a). On Being a Recognizable Indian Among Indians. In D. Carbaugh, Ed., *Cultural Communication and Intercultural Contact*. Hillsdale, NJ: Lawrence Erlbaum, pp. 45–64.

D. Lawrence Wieder and Steven Pratt (1990b). On the Occasioned and Situated Character of Members' Questions and Answers: Reflections on the Question, "Is He or She a Real Indian?" In D. Carbaugh, Ed., *Cultural Communication and Intercultural Contact*. Hillsdale, NJ: Lawrence Erlbaum, pp. 65–75.

5.4 Discourses coming into and going out of existence

Saint Simeon Stylites (390 AD–459 AD) was an ascetic who lived for 37 years on a small platform on top of a pillar near Aleppo in Syria (Lent 2008). He inspired a six century-long practice of *stylitoe* or "pillar-hermits". When St Simeon got up on his pillar, people had to interpret what he was doing and who he was trying to be. They had not seen pillar hermits before. St Simeon was first.

However, there were precedents on which they could draw. They were aware of holy men and women who engaged in ascetic practices, practices of severe self-discipline for religious reasons. Even St Simeon himself had previously shut himself up for three years in a hut and later confined himself within a narrow space among the rocks in a desert. However, when crowds of people sought him out for guidance and prayers, he had a pillar, with a small platform at its top, constructed and climbed up and started the Discourse of pillar hermits, a Discourse that lasted 600 years with many participants.

Saint Simeon often preached from his pillar—as did later pillar hermits—and in his sermons, he spoke with a lack of fanaticism and stressed compassion. He seems even now, from his words, to have been a person who was neither crazy nor inhumane.

Saint Simeon became a saint, but if you tried pillar sitting today, you would be seen as mentally ill. The niche for pillar hermits is now long gone. Of course, it might come back, though I doubt it; however, for now, it is gone and you are out of luck if you want to be one. For St. Simeon to be a pillar hermit, people had to recognize and accept that he was one (and understand what it meant to be one) and others had to become one, too.

So, one key question in which we are interested is this: How, at a given time or place, can a person get recognized as being a certain kind (or type) of person, as having a certain sort of socially recognizable and meaningful identity, an identity that helps others make sense of what he or she is saying and doing?

5.5 Vernacular social languages

Discourses are about enacting and recognizing socially significant identities. Though Discourses are always about more than language, one way we enact identity is by using different varieties (styles) of language. We earlier called different varieties of language-in-use (dialects, registers, styles, idiolects) **social languages**. The social language we use in interaction signals both who we want to be taken for as we speak (our identity for this interaction) and who we want the listener to respond as (what identity we want the listener to assume or take on).

One important variety (social language) of any language is the **vernacular**. The vernacular is not so much a single social language as a set of related social languages. The vernacular is the variety of language people use when they are communicating as **everyday people**, not specialists or experts of any sort. Even if a person is a specialist of a certain sort—say a doctor or an avid gamer—they often communicate as everyday people not drawing on their specialist identity, but on their identities as family members, friends, peers, or fellow everyday people in everyday encounters.

The Discourse (identity) with which vernacular social language is associated I will call "the lifeworld Discourse". Our **lifeworld** (Habermas 1984) is composed of the contexts in which we speak and act as everyday people drawing on common knowledge and "common sense". We make claims in our lifeworld Discourse that are based on shared and "common" knowledge, not on knowledge we know as experts or specialists.

Different people, even in one and the same language like English, speak different varieties of the vernacular based on their dialect, culture, ethnic group, or social class. Furthermore, all people switch among more and less formal versions of the vernacular based on who they are speaking to or on how they want their listener to respond and react to them.

Let me give an example I have long used. Consider the following case of an upper-middle-class, Anglo-American young woman named "Jane," in her twenties, who was attending one of my courses on language and society. The course was discussing different social languages. During the discussion, Jane claimed that she herself did not use different language styles in different contexts, but, rather, was consistent from context to context. In fact, to do otherwise, she said, would be "hypocritical," a failure to "be oneself".

To support her claim that she did not switch her style of speaking in different contexts and for different conversational partners, Jane decided to record herself talking to her parents and to her boyfriend. In both cases, she talked about a story the class had discussed earlier, to be sure that in both contexts she was talking about the same thing.

In the story—a moral clarifications task used in psychology—a character named Abigail wants to get across a river to see her true love, Gregory. A river boat captain (Roger) says he will take her only if she consents to sleep with him. In desperation to see Gregory, Abigail agrees to do so. But when she arrives and tells Gregory what she has done, he disowns her and sends her away. There is more to the story, but this is enough for our purposes here.

Students in my class had been asked to rank order the characters in the story from the most offensive to the least. In explaining to her parents why she thought Gregory was the worst (least moral) character in the story, the young woman said the following:

To parents at dinner:
Well /
when I thought about it /
I don't know /
it seemed to me that Gregory should be the most offensive //
He showed no understanding for Abigail /
when she told him what she was forced to do //
He was callous //
He was hypocritical /
in the sense that he professed to love her/
then acted like that//

Earlier, in her discussion with her boyfriend, in an informal setting, she also explained why she thought Gregory was the worst character. In this context she said:

To boyfriend late at night:
What an ass that guy was /
you know /
her boyfriend //
I should hope /
if I ever did that to see you /
you would shoot the guy //

It was clear—clear even to Jane—that Jane had used two very different forms of language. The differences between Jane's two social languages are everywhere apparent in the two texts.

To her parents, she carefully hedges her claims ("I don't know", "it seemed to me"); to her boyfriend, she makes her claims straight out. To her boyfriend, she uses terms such as "ass" and "guy", while to her parents she uses more formal terms such as "offensive", "understanding", "callous", "hypocritical", and "professed". She also uses more formal sentence structure to her parents ("it seemed to me that ...", "He showed no understanding for Abigail, when ...", "He was hypocritical in the sense that ...") than she does to her boyfriend ("...that guy, you know, her boyfriend", "Roger never lies, you know what I mean?").

Jane repeatedly addresses her boyfriend as "you", thereby noting his social involvement as a listener, but does not directly address her parents in this way. In talking to her boyfriend, she leaves several points to be inferred, points that she spells out more explicitly to her parents (e.g., her boyfriend must infer that Gregory is being accused of being a hypocrite from the information that though Roger is bad, at least he does not lie, which Gregory did in claiming to love Abigail).

Jane's style of language to both her boyfriend and her parents is vernacular language, she is speaking as an everyday person to her boyfriend and parents. Yet her vernacular language to her parents is more formal in style than is her vernacular language to her boyfriend, which is quite informal. Of course, informality and formality is not a binary distinction, but a continuum. People can vary formality across a scale from very informal to very formal with varieties in between.

Jane's language to her parents does not require that they make as many inferences and it distances them as listeners from social and emotional involvement with what she is saying, while stressing, perhaps, their cognitive involvement and their judgment of her and her "intelligence". Her language to her boyfriend stresses, on the other hand, social and affective involvement, solidarity, and co-participation in meaning-making.

Jane is making visible and recognizable two different versions of *who* she is and *what* she is doing. In one case, she is "a dutiful and intelligent daughter having dinner with her proud parents (who are proud of, and paying for, her education)" and in the other case she is "a girlfriend being intimate with her boyfriend".

I should add that while people like Jane may talk at dinner this way to their parents, not all people do; there are other identities one can take on for one's parents, other social languages one can speak to them. And, indeed, Jane undoubtedly speaks differently to her parents in different contexts or when discussing different topics.

5.6 Language and class

Jane's language to her parents sounds very "school like" and "public", in the sense that it sounds like the language teachers and students use at school when discussing things such as books and school subject matter. It sounds, as well, like the sorts of highly explicit language people tend to use in public forums where they cannot assume a lot of personal or cultural shared knowledge. At first, this seems odd as a style one would use with one's parents. But it is a style of language that some social groups use to show respect for, and deference to, the listener, just as Jane's way of speaking to her boyfriend is a way of bonding with him and showing solidarity with him.

Consider now two other speakers using their vernacular in a situation where we would expect a more formal style of the vernacular because they are communicating to a person older than them whom they do not know well. They are being interviewed by a graduate student from a local university. Both these speakers are white and in middle school. One (Jeremy) is from a poor neighborhood in a post-industrial town where even working-class jobs are now scarce. The other (Karin) is from an upper-middle-class suburb in a wealthy area in the same state. Both these young people are white.

Jeremy
Jeremy is talking about how he feels about other groups in his town
... like colored people I don't, I don't like //
I don't like Spanish people //
most of 'em //
but I like, I like some of 'em //
Because like if you—
it seems with them /
like they get all the welfare and stuff //
Well /
well white people get it too /
and everything //
but, I just—
And then they think they're bad //
and they're like—
They should speak English too //
just like stuff like that //

Karin

Karin is talking about whether kids from poor areas and schools have as much chance
as her and her peers to succeed
Not as good as they would in a good school system //
It depends on—
I know that they probably don't //
If they don't have enough money /
they might not have enough to put into the school system //
and not—
may not be able to pay the teachers /
and, um, the good supplies and the textbooks and everything //
So maybe they wouldn't—
they probably wouldn't have the same chance //
But I believe that every person has equal chances /
um, to become what they want to be //

There are three interesting things we can note here. First, both young people are speaking to a graduate student not from their community and a person they do not know well. So, we expect a somewhat more formal style, one that stresses deference or distance over solidarity. At the same time, the female graduate student interviewing these young people shares a gender and her social class with Karin, but neither with Jeremy.

Second, we can note that Karin's style of language in this context sounds more "school like" than Jeremy's, though less so than Jane's language to her parents at dinner. What we see here are class-based differences in the use of the vernacular. People in conversation usually adapt their speech to the person with whom they are speaking. Karin is accommodating to the graduate student's academic identity and to the rather academic nature of the interview. Jeremy is not. We do not know, of course, whether he does not know how to accommodate to the graduate student's identity, does not know what it is, or does not wish to.

In any case, in the United States it is common that middle- and upper-middle-class speakers use formal styles that sound "school like" or "public" in their vernacular in certain situations, while some groups of people from below the middle class often do not. This school-like formal vernacular style represents an allegiance to, affiliation with, or an alignment with (and often a trust in) schools and public sphere institutions in society (Bourdieu 1988).

Jeremy is much less affiliated in his norms, values, and practices with school and middle class institutions than is Karin. And, indeed, the schools and other institutions in his community have been "left behind" to decay and are, in many respects, isolated from even nearby prosperous areas and institutions. Thus, he has no deep desire to affiliate with school and public institutions (like colleges) in how he speaks to someone he does not know well and whose background, gender, and class are very different from his.

Third, we can note that both Jeremy and Karin contradict themselves. Jeremy condemns Hispanics for taking welfare, but concedes white people take it too. Karin says that kids from poor schools "probably wouldn't have the same chance", but then goes directly on say "[b]ut I believe that every person has equal chances to become what they want to be".

This shows two important aspects of everyday speech and interactions. First, as we have said above, when we use language we express perspectives on reality, based on the grammatical choices we have made, not just straight unmediated unvarnished truth. Like all of us, Jeremy and Karin are focused on expressing their perspective and not always on monitoring for "logical consistency". After all, both these young people are monitoring their interactive social relationship with the interviewer as much and, perhaps, more than they are monitoring their speech for logical consistency. They have quite a heavy cognitive load in this type of interview situation.

Here are my hypotheses as to why each speaker expressed a contradiction. I do not know for sure these hypotheses are true, though there are a good deal of data from the study in which these interviews were conducted to support them. Jeremy, I suspect, knew, at some level, that expressing hostile views about a minority to a college graduate student (from a private and high prestige university in his town) might be problematic, so he concedes that white people are, perhaps, really no better, while still venting his dislike of minorities and his anxiety that they will be advantaged over him (he elsewhere expresses his concerns about affirmative action), a person who is by no means well positioned for success in mainstream US culture.

Karin is wealthy and she is quite focused on getting into a good college. She is aware that her school is full of kids who go on to top high schools and colleges. Yet, she realizes, at some level, that her concession that poor kids' schools put them at an unfair disadvantage in comparison to her calls into question her own merit (that she has fairly earned her success) and also calls into question a very common American cultural belief that "anyone who tries hard enough can make it", a belief that, in fact, can help her feel better about the whole situation (after all, most people do not want to feel their success was unfairly achieved at the cost of other people).

Finally, these examples show us, along with a good deal of research on this topic, that speaking in a school-like formal version of the vernacular—a variety that many people associate with "educated people"—is not a guarantee whatsoever of logical consistency (Labov 1969). We are all, when we communicate, often more focused on identity and perspectives, than on logic and fact, no matter the degree of our education.

Recommended reading

Penelope Eckert (2000). *Linguistic Variation as Social Practice*. Oxford: Blackwell.
Lesley Milroy (1987). *Language and Social Networks*. Second Edition. Oxford: Blackwell.

5.7 Academic specialist social languages

Different versions of vernacular language are one big category of social languages. Another big category is what I will call **specialist social languages**. People use specialist social languages when they are speaking as specialists or experts of certain sorts, not just as everyday people. Specialist social languages fall into two big subcategories: academic social languages, which are used in academic contexts, and non-academic specialist languages used by specialists or experts in areas beyond academics.

Let me give an example of academic social languages at work, an example taken from Greg Myers' work (see Myers 1990; all page numbers below refer to this work). Biologists, and other scientists, write differently in professional journals than they do in popular science magazines. These two different ways of writing do different things and display different identities. The popular science article is *not* merely a "translation" or "simplification" of the professional article.

To see this, consider the two extracts below, the first from a professional journal, the second from a popular science magazine, both written by the same biologist on the same topic (p. 150):

Experiments show that *Heliconius* butterflies are less likely to oviposit on host plants that possess eggs or egg-like structures. These egg-mimics are an unambiguous example of a plant trait evolved in response to a host-restricted group of insect herbivores. (Professional journal)

Heliconius butterflies lay their eggs on *Passiflora* vines. In defense the vines seem to have evolved fake eggs that make it look to the butterflies as if eggs have already been laid on them. (Popular science)

The first extract, from a professional scientific journal, is about the *conceptual structure* of a specific *theory* within the scientific *discipline* of biology. Here we have a professional biologist writing for other professional biologists.

The subject of the initial sentence is "experiments", a *methodological* tool in natural science. The subject of the next sentence is "these egg-mimics": note how plant parts are named, not in terms of the plant itself, but in terms of the role they play in a particular *theory* of natural selection and evolution, namely "coevolution" of predator and prey (i.e., the theory that predator and prey evolve together by shaping each other). Note also, in this regard, the earlier "host plants", in the preceding sentence, rather than the "vines" of the popular passage.

In the second sentence, the butterflies are referred to as "a host-restricted group of insect herbivores", which points simultaneously to an aspect of scientific methodology (like "experiments" did) and to the logic of a theory (like "egg-mimics" did). Any scientist arguing for the theory of coevolution faces the difficulty of demonstrating a causal connection between a particular plant characteristic and a particular predator when most plants have so many different sorts of animals attacking them. A central methodological technique to overcome this problem is to study plant groups (like *Passiflora* vines) that are preyed on by only one or a few predators (in this case, *Heliconius* butterflies). "Host restricted group of insect herbivores", then, refers both to the relationship between plant and insect that is at the heart of the theory of coevolution and to the methodological technique of picking plants and insects that are *restricted* to each other so as to "control" for other sorts of interactions.

The first passage, then, is concerned with scientific methodology and a particular theoretical perspective on evolution. On the other hand, the second extract, from a popular science magazine, is not about methodology and theory, but about *animals* in *nature*. Here we have a professional biologist writing for an educated "lay" audience.

The butterflies are the subject of the first sentence and the vine is the subject of the second. Further, the butterflies and the vine are labeled as such, not in terms of their role in a theory. The second passage is a story about the struggles of insects and plants that are transparently open to the trained gaze of the scientist. Also, the plant and insect become "intentional" actors in the drama: the plants act in their own "defense" and things "look" a certain way to the insects, they are "deceived" by appearances as humans sometimes are.

These two examples replicate in the present what, in fact, is a historical difference. In the history of biology, the scientist's relationship with nature gradually changed from telling stories about direct observations of nature to carrying out complex experiments to test complex theories. Myers argues that professional science is now concerned with the expert management of uncertainty and complexity, and popular science is concerned with the general assurance that the world is knowable by, and directly accessible to, experts.

The need to "manage uncertainty" was created, in part, by the fact that mounting "observations" of nature led scientists, not to consensus, but to growing disagreement as to how to describe and explain such observations (seeing might be believing, but it is not knowing). This problem led, in turn, to the need to convince the public that such uncertainty did not damage the scientist's claim to professional expertise or the ultimate "knowability" of the world.

This example lets us see that ways with words are connected to different identities and their concomitant Discourses (here the biologist as experimenter/theoretician versus the biologist as a careful observer of nature) and activities within those Discourses (the professional contribution to science and the popularization of it). They also let us see that social languages are always engendered and licensed by specific social and historically shaped practices (activities) representing the *values* and *interests* of distinctive groups of people (Biber 1995).

Recommended reading

Michael A. K. Halliday (1978). *Language as Social Semiotic: The Social Interpretation of Language and Meaning*. London: Edward Arnold.

5.8 Non-academic specialist languages

Specialist languages exist not just in academics and in professions like law and medicine, they are proliferating outside such formal institutions in popular culture. People with interests in everyday activities such as gardening, gaming, cooking, birding, hip-hop, and many other activities have their own special ways with words that help them engage in their activities. Some of these non-academic specialist languages can get quite complicated, as complicated as academic and professional social languages (Gee 2004, 2007; Gee & Hayes 2011).

For example, consider *Yu-Gi-Oh*. *Yu-Gi-Oh* is a Japanese anime (Japanese animation) produced in books, films, television shows, and in a card game. The card game (structured much like *Magic: The Gathering*, another well-known card game) involves enacting the sorts of battles and stories that are seen in the books, films, and television shows. The rules of the game, which is played by two players, are quite complicated and the language of the rules and on each card is clearly "specialist" in the sense that people who are new to *Yu-Gi-Oh* have no real idea what it means, though they can certainly recognize the words. But they do not know what the words mean in the context of *Yu-Gi-Oh* as an activity.

Below I have reprinted one of the thousands of *Yu-Gi-Oh* cards and a short statement of one of the rules of the game:

Card

Cyber Raider
Card-Type: Effect Monster
Attribute: Dark | Level: 4
Type: Machine
ATK: 1400 | DEF: 1000
Description: When this card is Normal Summoned, Flip Summoned, or Special Summoned successfully, select and activate 1 of the following effects: Select 1 equipped Equip Spell Card and destroy it. Select 1 equipped Equip Spell Card and equip it to this card.

Rules

In order to Synchro Summon a Synchro Monster, you need 1 Tuner (look for "Tuner" next to its Type). The Tuner Monster and other face-up monsters you use for the Synchro Summon are called Synchro Material Monsters. The sum of their Levels is the Level of Synchro Monster you can Summon. (http://www.yugioh-card.com/lat-am/rulebook/YGO_RuleBook_EN-v8.pdf)

We can note, from the card, that *Yu-Gi-Oh* cards involve a complex classificatory system where players must know for several different attributes what category the card is in when compared to other cards (e.g., card type = effect monster). *Yu-Gi-Oh*, with its complex language and classificatory schemes, seems pretty "academic". Yet it is easily acquired and played, even by seven-year-old children, as well as older people, if they want to play the game. In fact, it is an interesting question to ask why language as specialist and complex as *Yu-Gi-Oh* seems to be easy to acquire for those with the desire, but academic language in school seems so daunting to many students.

Complex non-academic specialist social languages are proliferating out of school and outside formal institutions as digital and social media allow a very wide range of new activities, interests, and passions that people can share and develop into expertise (e.g., blogging, making videos, modding video games, engaging in activism, and so forth).

5.9 Authorship

When someone speaks or writes we take them to be the "author" of their words. But authorship is often far more complicated. Consider the two texts in Section 5.7 about *Heliconius* butterflies. These both came from—were attributed to the same scientist—writing for a journal in one case and a popular science magazine in the other. However, as anyone who has written for a magazine knows, the editors rewrite what you give them, often in major ways. They know the sort of language and information their readers expect to see and they ensure that what the "author" writes takes that form. I (Gee 2003) once had a short piece appear in *Wired* magazine (a prestigious popular magazine devoted to new media and technology). After going through several cycles of the editors rewriting my text, there was precious little left of what I had originally written. Most of the piece was now in the editors' words. Nonetheless, I alone was listed as the author. In reality the piece was written by the magazine using my ideas, but in the end, few of my actual, especially more academic, words (which, of course, affects the ideas as well).

But then, what about the scientist's piece in the professional journal? Journal editors and reviews do suggest revisions, but how you phrase them is usually up to you, the author. So, it seems clear that in the first example the scientist, with a little help, authored the piece? But, did he? The piece is written in a way that is strongly influenced by how the author's academic discipline demands the piece be written and follows closely how other biologists in his area of specialty write journal articles. The piece, in reality, was coauthored by the scientist and his subdiscipline in biology (that is, by his Discourse).

To see more clearly what it means to say the scientist's journal article was coauthored with his biological Discourse, consider the two sentences below. The first is in the vernacular (everyday language) and the second is in the language of a certain form of biology:

1a. Hornworms sure vary a lot in how well they grow
1b. Hornworm growth exhibits a significant amount of variation

Note that in (1a), if we ask on what basis the speaker claims hornworms vary a lot, the answer is his or her own experience with hornworms, perhaps ones that were part of a school project or a hobby at home. But if we ask of (1b) on what basis does the speaker (or writer) claim that hornworms display a significant amount of variation, the answer is not (just or really) his or her observations of hornworms, but that the academic subdiscipline from which the person is speaking has developed certain sorts of tests of significance that determine what counts as significant variation and the hornworm data (not the hornworms themselves) have passed the test.

In (1a) the speaker stands behind his or her claim. In (1b) the Discourse stands behind it and the scientist has come to give us the news. Now, one might ask whether there is any social contribution to the authorship in (1a) or whether we have finally found a case where the human being is the sole author. We pointed out above that when we speak as everyday people, not as specialists of any sort, we are speaking out of our lifeworld Discourse. When we speak out of our lifeworld Discourse we draw, however consciously or unconsciously, on what constitutes, in our time and place and culture, "common sense", "common knowledge", and "normal" ways of saying things. So, here too, even in (1a), when someone speaks as an everyday person, "just themselves", what they say is coauthored by a Discourse (a way of being and enacting an identity in the world), their socially and culturally specific lifeworld Discourse.

Recommended reading

Mikhail Bakhtin (1981). *The Dialogic Imagination*. Austin, TX: University of Texas Press.

Mikhail Bakhtin (1986). *Speech Genres and Other Late Essays*. Austin, TX: University of Texas Press.

References

Appiah, K. A. (2005). *The Ethics of Identity*. Princeton, NJ: Princeton University Press.

Biber, D. (1995). *Dimensions of Register Variation: A Cross-Linguistic Comparison*. Cambridge: Cambridge University Press.

Bourdieu, P. (1988). *Language and Symbolic Power*. Cambridge: Polity.

Gee, J. P. (2003). Games, Not School, Are Teaching Kids to Think. *Wired*, May 2003, pp. 91–92.

Gee, J. P. (2004). *Situated Language and Learning: A Critique of Traditional Schooling*. London: Routledge.

Gee, J. P. (2007). *What Video Games Have to Teach Us About Learning and Literacy*. Second Edition. New York: Palgrave/Macmillan.

Gee, J. P. (2014). Tools of Inquiry and Discourses. In A. Jaworski & N. Coupland, Eds., *The Discourse Reader*. Third Edition. New York: Routledge, pp. 142–153.

Gee, J. P. (2015). *Social Linguistics and Literacies: Ideologies in Discourses*. Fifth Edition. London: Taylor and Francis. Originally published 1990.

Gee, J. P. & Hayes, E. R. (2011). *Language and Learning in the Digital Age*. London: Routledge.

Habermas, J. (1984). *Theory of Communicative Action: Reason and the Rationalization of Society*, Vol. I, trans. by T. McCarthy. Boston, MA: Beacon Press.

Hacking, I. (2006). Making Up People. *The London Review of Books* 28.16: 23–26.

Labov, W. (1969). The Logic of Non-Standard English. *Georgetown Monograph on Languages and Linguistics* 22: 1–44.

Lent, F. (2008). *The Life of Saint Simeon Stylites: A Translation of the Syriac Text in Bedjan's Acta Martyrum Et Sanctorum*. Pennsauken, NJ: Arx.

Martin, E. (2007). *Bipolar Expeditions: Mania and Depression in American Culture*. Princeton, NJ: Princeton University Press.

Mishler, E. (2000). *Storylines: Craftartists' Narratives of Identity*. Cambridge, MA: Harvard University Press.

Myers, G. (1990). *Writing Biology: Texts in the Social Construction of Scientific Knowledge*. Madison, WI: University of Wisconsin Press.

Padden, C. A. & Humphries, T. L. (2005). *Inside Deaf Culture*. Cambridge, MA: Harvard University Press.

Taylor, C. (1989). *Sources of the Self: The Making of the Modern Identity*. Cambridge: MA: Harvard University Press.

Taylor, C., Appiah, K. A., Habermas, J., Rockefeller, S. C., Walzer, M., Wolf, S., & Gutmann, A. (1994). *Multiculturalism: Examining the Politics of Recognition*. Princeton, NJ: Princeton University Press.

6

Connections and discourse organization

6.1 Connections

When we put together two or more clauses into a single sentence we are integrating information, packing it together, as in (1a) below. When we separate information into separate sentences we are disaggregating, separating, pulling apart this information into separate "main thought" units (sentences), as in (1b):

1a. (When Mary walked out), (John thought (she would never return), (because she was very angry)) = 4 clauses/1 sentence
1b. Mary walked out. She was very angry. John thought (she would never return). 4 clauses/3 sentences

(1a) packages four clauses into one sentence. When clauses are packaged into one sentence, the connections among them are signaled by syntax (e.g., subordinate and embedded clauses) and grammatical words such as "when" and "because". In (1b) the same four clauses are distributed among three separate sentences and connections across these three sentences are signaled by words and phrases that relate to each other across the separate sentences (these are discourse connections).

In (1b) the pronoun "she" in "She was angry" signals a connection back to Mary in the first sentence, as does the "she" in "she would never return". "Mary ... she ... she" constitutes a chain of connections. Pronouns can make connections within a single sentence or across two or more separate sentences. There is also a connection made by the lexical pair "walk out" and "return", since these are opposites and one implies the other or raises questions about the other.

Below I give an example that we will discuss further. Each line is one intonation unit and I have bolded the focus stress (the one most important piece of new information in the unit):

1a. I **believe** in that (one clause)
1b. Whatever's gonna happen is gonna **happen** (two clauses)
1c. I believe that y'know it's **fate** (two clauses)
1d. It **really** is (one clause).

Each intonation unit here is one or two clauses long. When a unit is two clauses it is composed of very short clauses that are very closely connected to each other. In (1b) "Whatever's gonna happen" is the subject of "is (gonna happen)" and in (1c) "that … it's fate" is the object of "believe". "Y'know" is an interjection.

Note how connections are signaled across these units. (1b) spells out what "that" in (1a) means, while "fate" in (1c) names what this thing ("that") is. (1d) means "it really is fate", but has left out the word "fate" because it was used in (1c) and this omission is way to connect (1c) and (1d). Connections like this signal to the hearer that the four intonation units belong together and are about one topic. These connections signal that these four units are one bigger unit that is made up of the four intonation units. We will call such bigger units **stanzas** and discuss them further below.

In writing, we could write the above speech as four separate sentences, thus mimicking how the words were said. Or we could combine them into one sentence in various ways, such as:

2.   I believe that fate determines that whatever is going to happen is bound to happen

The example (1a–d) above from speech is more redundant than many forms of writing and some other forms of speech. One could have just said: "I believe everything happens for a reason". The reason for this redundancy, we will see below, is that the speaker is trying to do more than make concise claims or give explicit information. She is trying to make sense of, and cope with, the death of her father near the time of her marriage.

6.2 Speech sentences

One problem we face here, though, is this: While it is easy to tell what a sentence is in writing, it is much harder to tell what a sentence is in speech.

The main utterance unit in speech is what we will have called an idea unit, which is also an intonation unit.

While some linguists do not believe that sentences exist in speech—that they are only creatures of writing—I believe that the notion of a sentence is relevant and important to speech. I will define a **speech sentence** to be any set of one or more intonation units that ends on a **final intonation contour** and that together could constitute a sentence in writing thanks to how the parts are syntactically related. By a "final contour" and "non-final contour" I mean:

Final intonation contour (represented by "//")

An utterance said with a noticeable rise or fall (or rise–fall or fall–rise) of the pitch of the voice on the focus stress (the highest stressed word in an intonation contour). This sounds "final", as if a piece of information is "closed off" and "finished". This is like a period in writing.

Non-final intonation contour (represented by "/")

An utterance said with only a small rise or fall (or rise–fall or fall–rise) or a level pitch of the voice on the focus stress in the intonation contour. This sounds "non-final", as if more connected information is to come. This is like a comma in writing.

To see how this works, consider another part of the speech data that we will look at in more detail below:

1a. And I just felt /
1b. that move was meant to be /
1c. because if not /
1d. he wouldn't have been there //
1e. So y'know it just s- seems that that's how things work //

Each line is an idea unit and an intonation unit. However, note that the grammar of lines (1a–e) connects them in a way that they could constitute a sentence in writing: I just felt that move was meant to be, because if not he wouldn't have been there. Note, too, the speaker has placed non-final contours on all the intonation units until line (1d) where the speech sentence ends. If the speaker had placed a final contour at the end of line (1b), we would have had the following two speech sentences: "I just felt the move was meant to be. Because if not, he wouldn't have been there". Line (1e) is both a single intonation unit and a speech sentence (So it just seems that's how things work out).

Not all speech makes speech sentences clear and easy to find and there are forms of speech where the notion of a sentence may be irrelevant. But often speech sentences are easy enough to find, allowing, of course, for some cases that are unclear or harder to demarcate. Having said all this, I will now freely use the word "sentence" for both speech and writing.

6.3 Cohesion

We have seen that speakers and writers can make connections within and across sentences by using devices like pronouns to link things together. Such connecting devices are called **cohesion markers**. Halliday and Hasan (1976), in an important book about cohesion, argued that there are six major types of cohesive markers. Consider the two sentences below in (1) and the six types of cohesion beneath it:

1. The boss expected employees to contribute to his favorite charity. However, though most of them did, the part-time workers never would ___.

Pronouns. The pronoun the "them" in the second sentence links back to the preceding sentence by picking up its reference from a phrase in that sentence ("employees").

Determiners and quantifiers. The quantifier "most" in the second sentence links to the preceding sentence by indicating that we are now talking about a part ("most") of a whole that was talked about in the preceding sentence ("employees"). The determiner "the" in front of "part-time workers" links to the preceding sentence by indicating that the information it is attached to ("part-time workers") is information that is assumed to be predictable or known on the basis of the preceding sentence. In this case, it is predictable because the preceding sentence mentioned employees and part-time workers are types of employees.

Substitution. The word "did" substitutes for (stands in for) "contribute to his favorite charity" in the previous sentence. This allows us both not to repeat this information and to signal that the second sentence is linked to the preceding one.

Ellipsis. The blank after "never would" indicates a place where information has been left out (elided) because it is totally predictable based on the preceding sentence (the information is "contribute to his favorite charity"). Since we reconstruct the left-out information by considering the preceding sentence this ellipsis is a linking device.

Lexical cohesion. The word "worker" is lexically related to "employee" since workers are a type of employee. This links the two sentences together through the fact that they contain words that are semantically related.

Conjunctions and other conjunction-like links. The word "however" signals how the hearer is to relate the second sentence to the first. "However" introduces a sentence that contrasts with or contradicts something that has been said in a previous sentence

Recommended reading

Michael A. K. Halliday and Ruqaiya Hasan (1976). *Cohesion in English*. London: Longman.

6.4 Transcription

One reason speakers use cohesion markers is to make connections to signal what information is meant to go together as part of (or a sub-part of) a topic, theme, or argument. To see how this works we will investigate an everyday vernacular language argument in which a speaker (a young lower-middle-class woman from Philadelphia) defends her belief in fate in the face of tragedy.

Before we start, though, we need to get clear on a terminological problem. We call bounded pieces of written language—with a clear beginning and end—"texts". There is no equivalent word for speech. In speech data, it is often not clear what is the beginning and the end—and this can be true of some written data as well. We analysts sometimes just must make a choice to study a reasonably coherent passage of speech and writing and simply decide what, for our purposes, we will count as a beginning and end. I am going to use the word "text" for both speech and writing and mean by it a bounded stretch of language data that, for a given purpose, we take to be a whole with a (sometimes arbitrarily chosen) beginning and end.

Thus, we could study a part of a chapter in a novel or a part of a dinner-time conversation and count what we are studying as our text. In many cases, however, there are good reasons to count a stretch of speech or writing as a unified text with a clear beginning and end, because the language in this stretch "hangs together" to constitute a recognizable genre, such as an argument, story, explanation, novel, or journal article (or the methods section of the journal article).

When English speakers wish to communicate an extended amount of material, they must break it up into what I will call **lines** and **stanzas**. Lines are idea units/intonation units, which are often, but not always, one clause long. Stanzas are sets of lines about a single minimal topic, organized rhythmically and connected so as to hang together in a particularly tight way.

The stanza takes a perspective on a character, action, event, claim, or piece of information. Each stanza has a point of view such that when character, place, time, event, or the function of a piece of information changes (whether in an argument, report, exposition, or description), the stanza must change (see also Scollon & Scollon 1981, pp. 111–121). I will discuss lines and stanzas in more detail later. Lines and stanzas are part of what I will call **macrostructure**.

I print below an argument in terms of its lines and stanzas, numbering both for ease of reference later:

An argument within a conversation
  Stanza 1: Position to be argued for
1. I believe in that //
2. Whatever's gonna happen is gonna happen //
3. I believe ... that ... y'know it's fate //
4. It really is //
  Stanza 2: Support for position by giving personal experience
5. Because eh my husband has a brother /
6. that was killed in an automobile accident /
7. And at the same time there was another fellow /
8. in there /
9. that walked away with not even a **scratch** on him //
  Stanza 3: Position to be argued for (repeated)
10. And I really fee—
11. I don't feel y'can push fate /
12. and I think a lot of people do //
13. But I feel that you were put here for so many /

14. years or whatever the case is /
15. and that's how it is meant to be //
    Stanza 4: Support for position by giving personal experience
16. Because like when we got married /
17. we were supposed t'get married uh: like about five months later //
18. My husband got a notice t'go into the service and we moved it up //
19. And my father died the week … after we got married //
20. While we were on our honeymoon //
    Stanza 5: Conclusion: Position to be argued for (repeated)
21. And I just felt /
22. that **move** was meant to be /
23. because if not /
24. he wouldn't have been there //
25. So y'know it just s- seems that that's how things work //
(Text from Schiffrin 1987, pp. 49–50. Stanza markings are my own.)

In the transcript above, a double slash ("//") at the end of a line stands for a final contour (a closure contour), that is, a movement in the pitch of the voice that signals that an idea is considered by the speaker to be complete, closed off, finished. A single slash ("/") at the end of a line, on the other hand, stands for only a slight fall or rise in pitch, that is for a non-final contour ("a continuation contour"). Such a pitch movement signals that the information in a line is considered by the speaker to be not closed off or finished, but is intended to be supplemented by information that is to follow. Whether information is finished or in need of supplement is not a matter that is determined by the nature of the information itself, rather it is a decision (choice) that the speaker makes in rhetorically structuring her text to achieve the viewpoint she wishes.

Almost all linguists transcribe speech in terms of intonation units. Not all use stanzas, though they all acknowledge that speech often has units larger than a single intonation contour. Stories have parts like beginnings, middle, and ends; arguments can be composed of subarguments in service of a larger argument; conversations can have subtopics within a larger topic. Just as writing has paragraphs and sections and chapters, speakers must signal somehow what the larger coherent and meaningful parts of any extended talk are.

In the (speech) text above, the symbol "…" stands for a noticeable pause. The symbol ":" stands for extending the length of a sound. The symbol "-" stands for a truncated word (e.g., "s-) and the symbol "—" stands for a truncated intonational contour (e.g., "and I really fee—"). Bolding of a word (e.g., **move**) stands for emphatic stress.

A great deal has been written about transcription. There is no inherently right way to transcribe speech (but, for guides, see: DuBois, Schuetze-Coburn, Cumming, & Paolino 1992; Jefferson 2004). Discourse analysts always must make choices and these choices are often based on their theories and purposes. Transcripts are, in this sense, always theoretical. Furthermore, there is next to no limit on how many features of speech we can transcribe, especially because new audio and video and analytic technologies allow us to "see" progressively more in speech.

We can transcribe every pause from the shortest to the longest and even label them in terms of their exact length in seconds and milliseconds. We can transcribe speech overlaps between different speakers, intakes and outtakes of breath, eye gaze, hesitations, all sorts of speech fillers, laughter, anger, and different voice qualities and effects. For intonation contours, we can transcribe every fall and rise in the pitch of the voice from the smallest to the largest, as well as rise-falls and fall-rises in pitch. We can transcribe many different degrees of loudness and many different degrees of emphatic stress. All these features and more can be meaningfully relevant to speech.

As new technologies arise we will discover yet more speech signals that are relevant to meaning, however unconsciously, to speakers and hearers. But we have to stop some place. The more features of speech we transcribe, the longer and more detailed the transcript is, and the more we are in danger of missing the forest for the trees. The less we transcribe, the more we are in danger of missing the trees for the forest, though we can then handle larger stretches of data.

We discourse analysts have to make our choices based on our goals, theories, and what we believe is relevant. We need to recognize that transcribing more might always change our analysis and teach us something new—just as we can always consider more of the context in which speech happened and, perhaps, learn new things. But if we are to get on with our work—and engage in applying discourse analysis to real-world problems—we must make compromises and decisions, at least for a given time and project. There are times and projects where the forest is more important than the trees and times when the trees are. Indeed, that's why we need different types of discourse analysts and different types of discourse analysis, so we can make progress on several different fronts at once.

We can say that any transcription can be more or less "delicate". More delicate means transcribing more features of speech and less delicate means transcribing less features, with all sorts of degrees in between. My transcript above is pretty indelicate, though it could have been even less so for other purposes.

Recommended reading

E. Elinor Ochs (1979). Transcription as Theory. In E. Ochs and B. Schieffelin, Eds, *Developmental Pragmatics*. New York: Academic Press, pp. 43–71.

6.5 Analyzing an argument: Intonation units

So, let's turn to our argument made in speech. I reprint it again below:

An argument within a conversation
> *Stanza 1: Position to be argued for*
1. I believe in that //
2. Whatever's gonna happen is gonna happen //
3. I believe ... that ... y'know it's fate //
4. It really is //
> *Stanza 2: Support for position by giving personal experience*
5. Because eh my husband has a brother /
6. that was killed in an automobile accident /
7. And at the same time there was another fellow /
8. in there /
9. that walked away with not even a **scratch** on him //
> *Stanza 3: Position to be argued for (repeated)*
10. And I really fee—
11. I don't feel y'can push fate /
12. and I think a lot of people do //
13. But I feel that you were put here for so many /
14. years or whatever the case is /
15. and that's how it is meant to be //
> *Stanza 4: Support for position by giving personal experience*
16. Because like when we got married /
17. we were supposed t'get married uh: like about five months later //
18. My husband got a notice t'go into the service and we moved it up //
19. And my father died the week ... after we got married //
20. While we were on our honeymoon //

Stanza 5: Conclusion: Position to be argued for (repeated)
21. And I just felt /
22. that **move** was meant to be /
23. because if not /
24. he wouldn't have been there //
25. So y'know it just s- seems that that's how things work //(Text from Schiffrin 1987, pp. 49–50. Stanza markings are my own.)

People often think that everyday non-technical, informal argumentation is "irrational" in comparison with the more formal styles of argumentation found in schools and academic disciplines. We will see that everyday argumentation has deeper purposes than just validating a claim (winning a point) and that it is rational, but on its own terms.

Speakers do not just "say what they mean" and get it over with. They lay out information in a way that fits with their perspective on the information and the interaction. They are always communicating much more than the literal message. And to do this they use intonation, cohesion, and macro-structure. In discussing each of these below, I will try also to give some flavor for how they are mutually interconnected.

In this regard, consider in the above text lines 20 and 21 in Stanza 4:

1a. And my father died the week … after we got married //
1b. While we were on our honeymoon //

The speaker places each of these pieces of information into separate into-nation units each with a final contour. She could have used a non-final contour on the first of them to more closely connect the two pieces of information:

2a. And my father died the week after we got married /
2b. While we were on our honeymoon //

By placing an intonational full stop after each unit in (1), the speaker isolates and separates the two events (death and honeymoon), giving them equal prominence. In (2) the honeymoon is treated as simply a temporal background for the father's death, the foregrounded more prominent event in this case. At the level of meaning (1) and (2) are the equivalent of:

3. My father died the week after we got married. While we were on our honeymoon, can you believe it?

4. My father died the week after we got married while we were on our honeymoon.

The way the speaker has phrased her point (1) fits with the main theme of her argument. The father's death looks unconnected to the woman's honeymoon—just a coincidence, and, indeed, to the "rational" mind, these events are not connected. It's all an accident, so to speak. But the speaker's argument is that such a lack of connection is only apparent; at a deeper level, they are, in fact, connected by the workings of fate. The speaker's language in her argument, as we will see, constantly enacts and plays with the theme of connection and disconnection.

6.6 Analyzing an argument: Cohesion

Cohesion is the way in which the lines and stanzas of a passage are linked to or interrelated to each other. As we saw above, cohesion is achieved by a variety of linguistic devices, including conjunctions, pronouns, demonstratives, ellipsis, various sorts of adverbs, as well as repeated words and phrases. In fact, any word, phrase, or syntactic device that causes two lines to be related (linked together) makes for cohesion in the text. Such links are part of what stitches a passage together into a meaningful whole; they are like threads that tie language, and, thus, also, sense/meaning together.

We can see the operation of cohesion particularly clearly in how the word "because" functions in our text. Words like "because" have two functions in English; one is to tie two parts of a sentence together, the other is to tie two stanzas (or even larger parts of a text) together. Below I list the three uses of the word "because" in the passage:

Line 5: Because eh my husband has a brother /

Line 16: Because like when we got married /

Lines 21–24:   And I just felt /

that **move** was meant to be /

because if not /

he wouldn't have been there //

The word "because" in lines 21–24 is a typical intrasentential (within sentence) cohesive use of "because", simply connecting two clauses of a single "sentence" ("because if not he wouldn't have been there" is a subordinate clause). But the two other instances of the word "because" in this text are functioning differently. They are not intrasentential uses of cohesion, but rather what we might call interstanza uses.

Line 5 begins Stanza 2. Here "because" relates not two parts of a single sentence, but two stanzas (Stanzas 1 and 2); it is a discourse connector, not an intrasentential connector. "Because" here signals that Stanza 2 is support or evidence for the view expressed in Stanza 1, as we switch from the generalized language of personal belief and feeling in Stanza 1 to the narrative-based language of specific action and event in Stanza 2.

Stanza 3 returns to the generalized language of personal belief and feeling, whereas Stanza 4 again uses "because" (line 16) to introduce specific supporting data from action and event for the speaker's position. Thus, Stanzas 3 and 4 have a parallel structure to Stanzas 1 and 2: "general position (Stanzas 1 and 3); because specific case (Stanzas 2 and 4)", creating a large-scale parallelism that ties the passage together as a whole (helping to signal and develop its thematics).

These uses of "because" not only stitch the passage together, they help constitute its very sense: the brother's accident (in Stanza 2) and the wedding that has been moved forward in time (Stanza 4) are not just isolated events, as they at first seem, but rather the concrete, specific realizations of the generalized principles of fate (Stanzas 1 and 3).

6.7 Analyzing an argument: Discourse organization

Both the intonation units of the text and its cohesive devices contribute, along with its grammar and content, to the overall **discourse organization** of the text. By "discourse organization" I mean the organization of the text into lines and stanzas, as well as the way language patterns within and across these lines and stanzas. Stanzas and the larger parts of an argument or story composed of several stanzas (such as an introduction, or subargument, or episode in a story) constitute what we have called **macrostructure** (structure bigger than a sentence).

As we have seen, Stanza 1 states the general theme ("fate") in the generalized language of belief and feeling, while Stanza 2 exemplifies this theme in the specific narrative-based language of action and event. Stanza 3 returns to the generalized language of belief and feeling. Then, once again, Stanza 4 returns us to the specific narrative-based language of action and event. Stanza 5 concludes by returning to the more generalized language of belief and feeling about fate. The text, in deftly interweaving these two forms of language, makes its thematic "point": the world of concrete event and action is but a reflection (at a deeper level) of the generalized workings of "fate", workings open to feeling/belief, though not necessarily "reason".

We can look also at how language is distributed within and across the stanzas. Notice how Stanza 2 uses the passive voice ("was killed") and relative clauses to introduce the husband's brother and "another fellow" in a parallel fashion, thus "mimicking" the speaker's point that though their role in the accident was the same, fate capriciously treated them differently. One of the speaker's major themes is that what looks the same (connected) or different (unconnected) at a superficial level may be just the opposite at the "deeper" level of the workings of fate:

| my husband has | a brother | [that was killed] |
| there was | another fellow | [that walked away ...] |

6.8 Analyzing an argument: Contextualization

Speakers must signal to hearers what they take the context in which they are speaking to be and how they want their hearers to construe or construct that context in their minds. Since there are many elements that are part of any context, speakers must help hearers know which aspects of the context are relevant to the speaker's meanings and intention. The devices speakers use to help listeners make decisions about what the context is, how it should be construed, and which parts of it are most relevant are called **contextualization cues** (Levinson 2003).

Contextualization cues also help the hearer know what sort of person the speaker takes (or wants) the hearer to be for this communication, what sort of person the speaker takes herself to be for this communication, and what the speaker assumes the world (of things, ideas, and people) to be like for this communication. All these are both parts of the context.

We will look at the speaker's use of terms of feeling and belief, her use of the adverbs "really" and "just", as well of the ritualistic phrase "y'know" as contextualization signals. These elements set up a persona for the speaker, situate a place for the "appropriate" or compliant hearer, and signal a world within which the text makes sense and finds its grounding.

The first stanza just says literally "I believe in fate", but it says it in such a way that we know the speaker expects some skepticism on the hearer's part ("it really is"); that, nonetheless, she is forced to the view that she holds (repetition of "believe"); and that she knows that she is on sensitive ground, given the spiritual and metaphysical implications of her topic ("y'know" before "it's fate").

Stanza 3 returns to these themes: the "really" in "I really feel" in line 7 once again signals that the speaker is forced to her view, that she is tapping the wellspring of intuitive feeling beneath superficial levels of "rational" thought. In this stanza (Stanza 3) she goes on to repeat "I think" and "I feel", which together with "really", stresses her belief/feeling against not only superficial "rationality", but the implied skepticism of others who "push fate". In the concluding stanza, Stanza 5, the speaker once again uses the language of feeling, saying "I just felt that move was meant to be", the little word "just" setting up a tacit contrast of her basic and rationally inexplicable feelings as against an implied rationality that cannot explain such "coincidences".

To be a compliant hearer for this text (to accept its contextualization signals) is to adopt a sympathetic skepticism that is "overcome" in the face of the striking evidence offered by the speaker, in much the way the speaker herself is "forced" to acknowledge the workings of fate. We are in a world of (implied) contrasts between feelings and rationality, between the loose logic of the speaker's discourse-level *because*s and the stricter logic of science and rationality, though these latter are never explicitly named. A compliant hearer dare not advance that stricter logic and rationality. Such a move would only place the hearer with those who "push fate", and will run smack into the speaker's "that's just how I really feel".

The only "appropriate" place to "hear from" here is to accept the loose logic of the text, which is precisely the logic of fate, and, thus, the argument of the text. The concluding line says "it just seems that that's how things work out", and though "seems" is normally a term of implied doubt, this text has created a context in which what "seems" true (what I "just" or "really" feel/believe) is true. Thus, the "seems" in the last line is far from a term of doubt; it is here a term of "evidence" (the truth of what is "evident", "felt", "believed").

Recommended reading

John J. Gumperz (1982). *Discourse Strategies*. Cambridge: Cambridge University Press. (Gumperz invented the term "contextualization cue".)

6.9 Analyzing an argument: Thematic organization and contrasts

Many instances (but, of course, not all) of sense-making in language are organized around contrasts, usually binary contrasts (Culler 1982; Levi-Strauss 1979). These contrasts are signaled in a variety of ways by a speaker, including word and syntax choice, the use of discourse devices, and patterns of repetition and parallelism in the text. Creating contrasts is one way—there are others—of developing and organizing themes (main ideas) when we talk or write.

We have already seen that the text trades on an implied contrast of feeling/belief, on the one hand, and rational evidence, on the other (the latter never overtly named). We have also seen that it trades on the contrast between what appears to be unconnected and what is "really" connected at a deeper level by the workings of fate.

The text also works with the contrast between "and that's how it is meant to be" (line 12), which seems to imply a purpose or goal (an intention), and "whatever's gonna happen is gonna happen" (line 2), which seems to imply that things are determined to happen in a certain way, but to no set purpose or intention. This contrast is carried over in the ambiguity of "So y'know it just seems that that's how things work out" (line 21), which, in the context of the text, can mean either "things just happen mechanically" (the brother's death in Stanza 2) or "things work out for the best" (the father's presence at the wedding in Stanzas 4 and 5).

Within the contrasts which organize a text, often one side "wins out" over or "subordinates" the other. In our text, the "apparent" disconnection of events is subordinated to the "deeper" connection made by fate. The claims of "reason" (never explicitly allowed a voice in the text) are subordinated to the "basic" claims of feelings/beliefs (remember the workings of "really" and "just"). But, of course, it is this "winning out" here that allows this text to function as an "argument".

However, not uncommonly, this process of subordination of one side of a contrast to the other is "undermined" in the workings of the text. The "winning out" process is not fully resolved. The subordinated side raises its head uncomfortably, leaving us with a residue of paradox and/or contraction. The contrast in our text above, between intentional determination (well-intentioned determination, in fact) and mechanical determinism (the universe, like a clock, just works the way it works, once started), is an example.

The text clearly "attempts" to resolve this contrast in "favor" of intentional (well-intentioned) determination (things work out for the best) in that it ends on the presence of the father at the wedding before his death. But the resolution is not complete; we are still left with the "contradiction" between the brother's "ill fortune" and the father's "good fortune". Of course, the brother's "ill fortune" is the stranger's "good fortune" (who walked away unharmed from the accident). But this "relativity" of fate will undermine the whole argument of the text: if any event is "good fortune" from someone's perspective and "ill fortune" from someone else's, then fate is always "ill-intentioned" and "well-intentioned" at one and the same time, depending on the perspective from which we view (feel) it. This leads us directly into the hands of the deprivileged, subordinated side of the contrast: mechanical determination with no intention, good or bad, at all—or worse yet, subordinates both sides of the contrast to fate as fickle.

Such irresolutions exist in texts like ours precisely because, at a deeper level, such texts are attempts to come to terms with, to make sense of, very real paradoxes in life. In life, randomness and a universe indifferent to human desire play a much bigger role than we humans like to think. This was just the function Claude Levi-Strauss (1979) argued myth served in many cultures: to ease the pain of life and the randomness of the world. Though our text is not part of a traditional "myth system", it does trade on historically and socioculturally shared motifs, discourse devices, and themes. It, too, seeks to privilege one side of a contrast over another in order to "ease the pain". Many scholars have rightly stressed the role of stories and storytelling as a form of deep sense-making for humans, but humans use other genres—for example, here argument—to make deep sense of their experiences, as well.

6.10 The public work of understanding

When we speak, we must speak as some sort of *who* engaged in some sort of *what*. The listener, in order to engage in the work of interpretation, must know who the speaker is trying to be here and now. Is so-and-so speaking now as my doctor or my friend? As a fellow Native-American, as a fellow professional in a shared profession, as a "stranger"? Is so-and-so speaking as a scientist, an activist, an "everyday person" (trading on "common sense")? Is so-and-so speaking as a street gang member, a struggling student, or a civically concerned youth?

The listener, in order to engage in the work of interpretation, must also know what the speaker is trying to do here and how. Is so-and-so offering medical advice or personal help? Is so-and-so recruiting me to a cause or bonding to me as a friend? Is so-and-so trying to convince me in an argument or vent opinions that he, perhaps mistakenly, thinks we share? Is so-and-so trying to con me or authentically recruit my help?

Earlier, I used the term "Discourse" with a capital "D" ("big 'D' Discourses") to name specific ways of enacting or recognizing socially significant identities and their associated socially significant activities (or practices). A Discourse is a set of ways of speaking (writing), acting, interacting, valuing, dressing, using objects, tools, and technologies in specific sorts of places and at specific sorts of times in order to be recognized as enacting a socially significant identity. A Discourse is a dance with words, deeds, and things.

Being a birder, African-American, radical feminist, lawyer, gang member, biker, linguist, an "everyday person", graduate student, gamer (each of a certain sort or type) are all Discourses. In Ian Hacking's (1986) terms, Discourses are ways of enacting and recognizing certain "kinds of people". Discourses are not discrete units, but waves that can flow into each other, overlap, and align or conflict with each other. They are contestable, negotiable, and more or less flexible across different contexts. They change across time and appear and disappear across history.

In conversations speakers and listeners seek to align themselves with each other, to get and stay on the "same page" (Gee 2015; Weigand 2010). If two people are to align with each other in conversation, they must do so in part through recruiting enough shared experience to know what words and things can mean mutually to, and for, each other in terms of what identities and activities (practices) are relevant here and now. It is not just people that are aligning, but Discourses that are aligning (and communicating or miscommunicating with each other). When Harry talks to Sally, it might also be an instance of the Discourse of male tech-nerds communicating (or miscommunicating) with the Discourse of back-to-nature radical environmentalists or, perhaps, a graduate student communicating with a doctoral advisor in the Discourse of graduate school (in some disciplinary guise). We align with others both as individuals with our own unique life histories (trajectories through Discourses across time and space) and as Discourses (kinds of people) talking to each other.

Recommended reading

Mikhail Bakhtin (1981). *The Dialogic Imagination: Four Essays by M. M. Bakhtin.* Austin, TX: University of Texas Press. Originally published in 1934.

Ron Scollon and Suzanne W. Scollon (1981). *Narrative, Literacy, and Face in Interethnic Communication*. Norwood, NJ: Ablex. (One of the best books ever written on discourse, language, culture, and communication.)

6.11 Conversation

Now I want to give an example of how alignment and Discourses work in face-to-face conversation. Face-to-face conversation is a primordial and fundamental form of communication for humans. For most of our history as a species, long before writing was invented and digital media arose, we humans worked out our social relations, identities, status, solidarity, competition, and collaboration with others.

Below is a conversation that occurred after a formal meeting had ended and some people had left and others had stayed a while to "chat" face-to-face. The meeting had been a session of a project in which professors from a university and school teachers were working together to create an oral history curriculum for middle-school students. The professors and the teachers were in a post-industrial working-class town on the East Coast of the USA.

There were town-gown problems in the town and in the project, since the teachers were third-generation natives of the town who had used teaching to enter the middle class and the professors were mobile professionals at a private college, none of whom had been born in the town and, for the most part, intended to stay in it. There were also conflicts in the meetings at times due to differences between the Discourses of the college professors (in education and history) and middle-school teachers in the project.

In the transcript below, Sara is a professor of history and Carol and Janet are middle school teachers in the same school and friends. Joe is a curriculum coordinator at another middle school in town. Carol, Janet, and Joe are "natives" and Sara is not (she was born elsewhere and is now no longer there).

Carol:
1. My mother used to talk about in the 40s /
2. You'd hang around at Union Station/
3. And anybody would just pick you up /
4. Because everybody was going down to dance at Bright City /
5. Whether you knew them or not //
Joe:
6. Lakeside Ballroom //

Janet:

7. Yeah definitely //

Joe:

8. My father used to work there //

Janet:

9. And also, once you finally get into the war situation /

10. Because you have Fort Derby /

11. Everybody would get a ride in to come to Bright City /

12. To the amusement park //

13. So it was this influx of two, three cars worth of guys /

14. That were now available to meet the girls that suddenly were there //

Sara:

15. Well actually street, street cars had just come in in this /

16. And as I recall um from a student who wrote a paper on this /

17. Bright City and Park was built by the street car company /

18. In order to have it a sort of target destination for people to go to /

19. And to symbiotically make money off of this //

Janet:

20. Because once you got there /

21. You could take a boat ride /

22. And go up and down a lake /

23. And there were lots of other ways to get the money from people //

This "chat" follows a meeting in which the participants had been speaking as teachers and professors. Now Carol, Janet, and Joe are speaking as long-time "natives" of the town. They are bonding around their shared knowledge and history as natives, enacting their identities as such natives. They are speaking in their vernacular style of language as "everyday people" (they are speaking as part of what I earlier called their lifeworld Discourse) who share knowledge and experiences that make them the same or similar "kinds of people" in their identities as "natives".

This type of talk serves the purpose of expressing solidarity, bonding, and common belonging. For these teachers, this type of talk is important in their town. They are the product of a nearly two-century long pattern of "white" migration to Worcester, Massachusetts, once a solid and prosperous working-class town, but now economically depressed, as jobs have moved overseas, and the location of new widespread "brown" immigration from Asia, South America, and the Caribbean. They have nostalgia for their "better days" and a focus, both as natives and teachers, in bringing the town back and forging the new immigrants into "citizens of Worcester".

From lines 1–14 each speaker has overlapped and effortlessly continued the talk of the previous speaker. There are ways to transcribe such overlap, but here I will just stress how the first 14 lines are collaboratively produced, as each speaker appears to contribute to a shared past and a shared story. In a more formal analysis, a great deal could be transcribed from audio and video here to study the embodied nature of alignment in conversation.

Such a conversation puts Sara, a university historian, at a disadvantage, since she is not a native of Worcester and does not share the others' past and experiences as natives. When she attempts to participate, she cannot enact the identity of a native, but, nonetheless, she must somehow seek to align herself with the informal and bonding talk of the teachers.

Sara enacts her identity as a historian in the midst of this vernacular bonding talk. She uses "facts" from a paper and speaks just a bit away from the vernacular towards academic language (e.g., "target destination", "symbiotically", the passive construction in line 17). Sara is aligning with the natives in terms of content and topic (and by a mostly vernacular style of language), but is treating that content and topic not as shared memory but as text-based knowledge.

This attempt at alignment, in one way, does not work well. Sara's "well actually" sounds like she is correcting the natives' knowledge. Her remarks seem to imply that text-based evidence trumps oral evidence based on shared memories, an implication that does not sit well with a project in which Sara is helping the teachers to get their students to engage in oral history as a valid form of historical research and a valid source of evidential claims in history.

Sara's remark that the street-car company built Bright City and Park to make money is related to a common academic approach in which academics stress how systems (the macro level) often have properties that are not apparent on the ground level (the micro level) to the participants in these systems, who, in some sense, "mis-recognize" the workings or "intentions" of the system. What, for the natives, is a site of meet-ups for men and women (and resulted in many of the children of the next generation—and is, thus, part of the origin story of the natives)—becomes for Sara a part of the workings of institutions and capitalism.

In another way, though, Sara's bid to participate does work, because Janet "redeems" it. She does so by a common conversational move. Sara had changed the topic (from meet-ups to money) but continued to speak topically (by introducing new content in a way that still tied to and was introduced as relevant to the content of the previous topic, namely meet-ups at Bright City).

Janet, in turn, changes the topic back to the original one, but speaks topically by tying to and incorporating Sara's topic. Janet aligns "ways of making money" and the multiple activities at the park, all of which were part and parcel of the "dates" men and women had there as they bonded during the war. Janet's "And there were lots of other ways to get money from people" concedes Sara's point and, with the phrase "get money from people", picks up on Sara's implication that people were being "used" for profit or, in some sense, "duped" or manipulated.

Janet's move is quite possibly an example of courtesy and alignment to down-play conflict. I say this because in the project as a whole it was a common move for both the professors and the teachers to avoid conflict enough to get their common task accomplished. However, this sometimes meant mitigating, effacing, and not confronting genuine differences in values, epistemology, perspectives, and taken-for-granted assumptions. In this respect, "alignment" can sometimes become evasion, and a way of, ironically, perpetuating a lack of alignment, respect, and understanding among Discourses.

This example is interesting, as well, in that in this project there had been a continuous low-level conflict over who had the right to make claims, how, and on what basis. The professors favored claims based on texts, research, and academic theories; the teachers favored claims made based on their personal experiences as both natives of and teachers in Worcester. Rights to claim and know are often a source of conflict across Discourses.

The example is relevant as well to the workings of what sociologists call "face" (Scollon & Scollon 1981). Every human being has a "positive face", the face one orients towards others in seeking social interaction and a "negative face", the face one turns away from others when seeking privacy and a haven from social invasions. All of us have both a need for inclusion in social interaction and a need for the ability to choose to be outside social interactions that we may find imposing. Here, Sara's positive face needs are at stake. She wants to be part of the group here, but faces the possibility of rejection. Janet handles Sara's positive face needs here well, but Sara's contribution is, nonetheless, one element among many that, across the whole project, announce that she is an "outsider" to the teachers' Discourses and they to hers.

Recommended reading

Chris Argyris (1993). *Knowledge for Action: A Guide to Overcoming Barriers to Organizational Change*. Boston, MA: Jossey-Bass.

John Heritage and Steven E. Clayman (2010). *Talk in Action: Interactions, Identities and Institutions*. Boston, MA: Wiley-Blackwell.

References

Culler, J. (1982). *Deconstruction: Theory and Criticism after Structuralism*. 25th Anniversary Edition, 2005. Ithaca, NY: Cornell University Press.

DuBois, J., Schuetze-Coburn, S., Cumming, S., & Paolino, D. (1992). Outline of Discourse Transcription. In J. A. Edwards & Martin D. Lampert, Eds, *Talking Data – Transcription and Coding in Discourse Research*. Hillsdale, NJ: Erlbaum, pp. 123–148.

Gee, J. P. (2015). Reflections on Understanding, Alignment, the Social Mind, and Language in Use. *Language and Dialogue* 5.2: 300–311.

Hacking, I (1986). Making Up People. In T. C. Heller, M. Sosna, and D. E. Wellbery, with A. I. Davidson, A. Swidler, and I. Watt, Eds., *Reconstructing Individualism: Autonomy, Individuality, and the Self in Western Thought*. Stanford, CA: Stanford University Press, pp. 222–236.

Halliday, M. A. K. & Hasan, R. (1976). *Cohesion in English*. London: Longman.

Jefferson, G. (2004). Glossary of Transcript Symbols with an Introduction. In G. H. Lerner, Ed., *Conversation Analysis: Studies from the First Generation*. Amsterdam: John Benjamins, pp. 13–31.

Levi-Strauss, C. (1979). *Myth and Meaning*. New York: Schocken Books.

Levinson, S. C. (2003). Contextualizing 'Contextualization Cues'. In S. Eerdmans, C. Prevignano, & P. Thibault, Eds, *Language and Interaction: Discussions with John J. Gumperz*. Amsterdam: John Benjamins, pp. 31–39.

Schiffrin, D. (1987). *Discourse Markers*. Cambridge: Cambridge University Press.

Scollon, R. & Scollon, S. W. (1981). *Narrative, Literacy, and Face in Interethnic Communication*. Norwood, NJ: Ablex.

Weigand, E. (2010). *Dialogue: The Mixed Game*. Amsterdam: John Benjamins.

7

Narrative

7.1 The importance of narrative

Narrative, usually in the form of a story, is a primordial form of sense making. It has been with us humans from the beginning. Every culture uses narrative to share experience, bond together, and to story lives, events, and identities. Narrative is a core way human beings express perspectives on the world, often through images and actions that "stand for" deeper emotions and meanings.

Narrative is a form of language that orders events in time. Stories are narratives with plots. Each culture tells stories in different ways, but at heart storytelling is pan-human. We humans need to see meaning in what happens and the prime way we do this is to construct a story that makes sense of what has happened and that allows us to feel in control, to be hopeful, and not to be left in the darkness of randomness and happenstance.

In this chapter, I will discuss a girl I will call "Sandra" (not her real name), a white, working-class teenager. Sandra is an active and resilient participant in her environments, with no "special" problems untypical of those environments, though those environments present plenty of very real problems for teenagers like Sandra. Sandra lives in the same town in which the history project we discussed earlier took place, a post-industrial city facing a lack of jobs and opportunity. The town is also undergoing a major demographic change stemming from "brown" immigrants from Mexico, South America, Asia, and the Caribbean. These brown people have now joined white people who are the product of earlier waves of white immigration in the 19th century and African-Americans who were the product of the "freedom train" and escape from slavery even earlier.

Sandra was interviewed for a project on teenagers' life stories in this town. The interviewer was a middle-class white female graduate student earning a PhD in psychology. Sandra knew and trusted the interviewer because the interviewer had spent a good deal of time hanging out with teens in the town and showing a real interest in their lives.

Here I want to analyze one of many stories Sandra told in her interview. But first I want to set the analysis of this narrative in the larger context of Sandra's whole interview. I want to stress the ways in which an analysis of the rest of the interview and of this narrative can mutually support each other, helping us to achieve some degree of validity in terms of a criteria converging across all of our data.

Recommended reading

Catherine K. Riessman (1993). *Narrative Analysis*. Newbury Park, CA: SAGE.

7.2 Connections and motifs

We will start our analysis of Sandra's interview with how Sandra builds connections that help us know what she sees as connected and what she sees as disconnected. Our first step when we analyzed Sandra's interview was to look across the whole interview for themes, motifs, or images that colocate (correlate) with each other, that is, themes, images, or motifs that seem to "go together". Such related themes connect diverse parts of the interview together and give it a certain overall coherence and "texture". In doing so, they render certain things as connected and relevant to each other in Sandra's world, and other things as not as closely connected or relevant to each other.

There are three related motifs that run through Sandra's interview. All three of these motifs have to do with how Sandra sees things in her world as connected or disconnected, especially the latter. In fact, the notion of connection, and especially disconnection, is a major overall theme in Sandra's interview and world-view.

In the case of each motif, Sandra uses many words and phrases that appear to share certain aspects of situational meaning with each other. Below, I list some examples of each of these motifs under the labels "Disconnection," "Not Caring," and "Language and Laughter". These are Sandra's three major motifs. It is apparent that "Not Caring" is also a form of disconnection, and many of the "Language and Laughter" examples involve affective language, nonsense, noise, or laughter as ways to disconnect from authority and hurtful (judgmental) language. These three motifs constitute connected threads that run throughout Sandra's interview:

Motif 1: *Disconnection*: Examples: Sandra's boyfriend is blamed for things, but "like nothing happens, he don't get punished"; Sandra tells her father to "shove it," but "I don't get punished" (there is "no point since they are getting a divorce"); Sandra's best friend is punished by her father "for nothing"; her best friend's father makes her friend clean up a mess she didn't make; Sandra's boyfriend refuses to clean up a mess he made, but goes on to clean up the whole yard unasked; Sandra is "always in trouble for what she didn't do"; drunken neighbors give her too much money for babysitting; Sandra "forgets to forget" a babysitting appointment that had been canceled and shows up anyway, and the people go out anyway; Sandra emotionally "freaks out" at night, but doesn't really know why; Sandra wants no relationship with her parents because too good a relationship would be "weird"; Sandra was "supposed to have been a boy", but the adoption agency failed to tell her parents she was a girl; her mother punishes her sister without knowing what really happened; a friend tells her one of her favorite dresses is ugly and offers to take it to the Salvation Army, only to keep it for herself; Sandra's grandmother is the "thing she holds onto", but "she is kinda flaky lately"; Sandra's friends laugh at her at a party, but she can't understand what's so funny, she doesn't "get it at all".

Motif 2: *Not Caring*. Examples: Sandra's boyfriend swears and smokes and his "mom doesn't care"; he smokes weed and "nobody cares"; he was "on house arrest and he went out anyway"; Sandra and her friends blame her boyfriend for everything, but "he don't care"; Sandra "doesn't care" that "nobody likes him [her boyfriend]", nor that her father "hates" him [her boyfriend]; Sandra's best friend is adopted, but "she doesn't care"; Sandra's best friend writes on mirrors "and she doesn't care"; if people say she's a "slut", "it doesn't bother her".

Motif 3. *Language and Laughter*. Examples: Sandra's sister's fiancé says he hates her and then gives her a diamond ring; Sandra's sister's fiancé threatens her, but he "is only fooling around"; Sandra blurts out "shut up, you fart smellers" at a wedding party when people are looking at her and she doesn't know what to say; Sandra often says things like "pool pilter" instead of "pool filter"; people she cares about give her "the answer I want to hear, that sounds right, with my problem"; Sandra's grandmother says "weird funny" things to make her laugh, like "I smell you" rather than "I love you"; Sandra's oldest sister says something good "and then ruins it"; Sandra's best friend's mother is "cool" and "we talk to her" because she "buys cigarettes for people" and "she won't say nothin"; if someone says something to hurt her feelings, Sandra shakes until "someone says something to make me feel better"; Sandra's boyfriend and grandmother hold her to make her feel better, but her mother "says stupid things"; when Sandra confronts a white girl who "thinks she's black" and who has insulted Sandra, the girl puts her fist to Sandra's face and says "Talk to the hand, my face don't understand", and Sandra replies "If your hand had a mouth I'd talk to it"; Sandra likes her boyfriend because he's "funny" and "makes me laugh"; her best friend makes her laugh when she does funny stuff she doesn't realize she's doing; her best friend makes her laugh by making funny noises; her best friend makes her laugh by pretending to smoke in a way she really doesn't.

My interest in these themes is to use them to begin to form hypotheses about some of Sandra's situational meanings and perspectives on reality, hypotheses that I can then check by further consultation of this and other data. I also want to see how these motifs illuminate the narrative we are going to analyze below and how that narrative illuminates these motifs.

So, we see that Sandra uses a large number of words and phrases that take on, in her interview, situational meanings that cluster around the three motifs I have listed above. In turn, these motifs are all integrally concerned with building connections and disconnections in the world as Sandra sees it and portrays it in her interview. However, Sandra's third motif, the one we have labeled Laughter and Language, also relates to how Sandra thinks about knowledge and authority.

In Motif 3, in particular, Sandra seems to disavow the *representational* function between words and the world, the very language function that others (e.g., schools) take to be of primary importance. By "representational function" I mean the idea that language connects directly and straightforwardly ("objectively") to the world "out there" ("re-presents" it), and that this has little to do with how people feel, what their needs are, or what their personal opinions are.

Sandra sees words said only because they are "true", or are "facts" backed up by some authority figure (e.g., her sister, her mother, her father, or, by extension, her teacher), as "stupid" and as a way to "ruin" things. In turn, Sandra celebrates the social, bonding, and affective functions of language. Language that is silly or funny, but that "feels right" and that is intended to make one feel good, is the only truly efficacious language. Sandra wants to relate only to those who tell her "the answer I want to hear, that sounds right, with my problem". She wants a relationship with an adult only if they "won't say nothin'" (i.e., won't engage in judgmental language or tell on her), or if they speak "silly", but endearing talk to her, like her grandmother.

Sandra is privileging one form of language, namely affective, caring language, and dis-privileging another form, namely objective, unemotional, fact-giving, authoritative language. Of course, this also relates to ways of knowing the world and other people, as well as ways of relating to them, that Sandra either prefers or dis-prefers.

From our overall analysis of Sandra's interviews, we eventually drew the hypothesis that she was operating with a perspective something like this:

> Objective, fact-giving language, especially objective, fact-giving, judgmental language, is the preserve of "authority" figures, people who are often uncaring and untrustworthy. In contradistinction to such language, language that is used primarily for social bonding, and which speaks to people's emotional needs, and is not used primarily to give facts or make judgments, is the preserve of friends and people who are caring and trustworthy.

Sandra disavows "authoritative representation" (whether adult control or the authority of asocial "factual" language), both in terms of how her world is and in terms of her ways of being in that world. This disavowal is coupled with a celebration of social interaction outside of, or opposed to, such authoritative representation.

Once we have hypothesized this perspective as operative in Sandra's interview, we can gather more data about how far and widely it functions in her world. It is interesting, for example, to ask if and how it operates in her relationship to teachers and school. Evidence we collected on this score showed, in fact, that Sandra liked teachers who showed they cared about the students personally (e.g., a teacher who understood that a student was asleep in class because the student had been working at a job the night before) and disliked those who stressed academic content, but not caring.

7.3 Sandra's perspective

Let me give a final brief example that captures the perspective we have attributed to Sandra. In response to the interviewer's question "Is there someone ... who you feel really doesn't understand you?", Sandra breaks into a long story about taking a drive with her sister after she (Sandra) had been punished by her mother, where her sister clearly wanted to offer Sandra "authoritative" advice and to know "facts" about her life (e.g., in regard to boys and safe sex) outside of any ongoing social interaction ("She's never talked to me like that before"). While there are other parts of Sandra's interview where she talks freely about sex with her friends, her response here is, "Wow! That's weird".

The understanding Sandra wants from her sister—or anyone else, for that matter—is based on words that consider her affective (not cognitive) perspective, that are part and parcel of ongoing egalitarian social interaction, and that are used to heal and bond. Words outside such a context, "authoritative words", make "no sense". Thus, she says of her sister: "... she'll give me a right answer, like the answer that I want to hear, ... but then we'll keep talking about it, and it will make no more sense, no more sense". By this, Sandra means that the sister will start to answer in an empathetic and affective way, but then switch to more authority-based talk offering facts and adult advice.

In Chapter 9 below I will make a distinction between a perspective that certain grammatical choices express in a given situation and what we will call a "framework". A framework is like a theory. It is a set of connected claims and perspectives that hang together to express a larger viewpoint. This larger viewpoint then guides the expression of specific perspectives—connected to the overall theory or framework—in specific situations where we often see only part of the overall theory or framework. In Sandra's case, we are on the verge of uncovering a large framework about human relationships and social institutions.

7.4 Sandra's narrative

My main interest in this chapter is to see how our data and ideas about Sandra's motifs can illuminate and be illuminated by a close look at one of her narratives. Turning to one of Sandra's narratives allows us to get much closer to the details of her actual language and "voice".

At the beginning of her interview, Sandra brings up her boyfriend, and the interviewer asks, "What kind of boyfriend is he?"; Sandra responds with what sounds like a series of only loosely connected stories. However, Sandra's approach to narrative is classically "oral". Once we carefully consider the features of such storytelling, it becomes apparent that Sandra's seemingly multiple stories constitute one tightly organized unified story.

Sandra's story is reprinted below. I label its sub-stories and sub-sub-stories in terms that will become clear in the analysis to follow. In order to see the patterning in this narrative all the more clearly, I do something a bit different in the way I represent lines and stanzas. I remove from the girl's story the various sorts of speech hesitations and dysfluencies that are part and parcel of all speech (and that tell us something about how planning is going on in the speaker's head). I also place the girl's lines back into clauses when they are not full clauses.

Idealized lines are useful when we are interested in discovering meaningful patterns in people's speech and in getting at their basic themes and how they are organized. Using them does not mean that we have totally ignored the details of actual speech. In fact, we can use hesitations, pauses, dysfluencies, and non-clause lines as indicators of how planning is working, where stanza boundaries exist, and how the speaker views her information at a micro-level. In actual analyses, we can always shuttle back and forth between the actual lines and idealized lines.

STORY: THE RETURN OF THE TABLE
FRAME
Stanza 1

1. [Sighs] He's nice.
2. He's, he's, he like he's okay, like
3. I don't know how to explain it.
4. Like, say that you're depressed, he'd just cheer ya up somehow.
5. He would, he'd make ya laugh or somethin
6. And you can't stop laughin, it's so funny

SUB-STORY 1: BREAKING THINGS
SUB-SUB-STORY 1: BREAKING THE FAN
EXPOSITION
Stanza 2

7. Like he does these, like today his mom hit the, she she, he was, he was, he was arguing with his mom,
8. He swears at his mom and stuff like that,
9. He's like that kind of a person
10. And his mom don't care.

Stanza 3

11. He smokes,
12. His mom don't care or nothin,
13. He smokes weed and everything and nobody cares.
14. Cos they can't stop him,
15. He's gonna do it any way
16. Like on house arrest he went out anyway.

START OF SUB- SUB-STORY 1 PROPER
Stanza 4 [Started]

17. So they're like so yesterday he was arguing
18. And she held a rake
19. And she went like that to hit him in the back of the butt,

Stanza 5 [Expository Aside]

20. Like she don't hit him,
21. She wouldn't hit him
22. She just taps him with things,
23. She won't actually like actually hit him

Stanza 4 [Continued]

24. She just puts the rake like fool around wit' him,
25. Like go like that,
26. Like he does to her.

Stanza 6

27. Like he was, and like she was holding the rake up like this
28. And he pushed her
29. And the rake toppled over the um, fan.
30. It went kkrrhhh, like that.
31. And he started laughing,

Stanza 7 [Expository Aside]

32. And when he laughs, everybody else laughs
33. Cos the way he laughs is funny,

34. It's like hahahahah!
35. He like laughs like a girl kind of a thing.
36. He's funny.

Stanza 8

37. And then his mother goes, "What are you doing Mike?"
38. And she's like going, "What are you doing? Why are you laughing?"
39. And she goes, "Oh my god it broke, it broke!"
40. And she's gettin all, she's gettin all mad the fan's broken
41. And she trips over the rake,

Stanza 9

42. And she goes into the room
43. And she's like, "Don't laugh, don't laugh",
44. And he keeps laughin.
45. It's just so funny.

SUB-SUB-STORY 2: BREAKING THE TABLE
EXPOSITION
Stanza 10

46. And he'll knock down the table
47. And he'll, like we'll play a game,
48. It's me, Kelly and him and Kelly's boyfriend,
49. It's just kinda fun
50. Cos it's just weird,

Stanza 11

51. We like don't get in trouble,
52. Like he gets blamed for it,
53. Like nothing happens.
54. He don't get punished.

Stanza 12

55. So we always blame him for everything.
56. He don't care,
57. He says, "go ahead, yeah, it doesn't matter."

START OF SUB-SUB-STORY 2 PROPER
Stanza 13

58. So we were pulling the table
59. And he was supposed to sit on it, jump on it and sit on it
60. And he didn't,
61. He missed

Stanza 14

62. And the table went blopp! over
63. And it broke.
64. Like it's like a glass patio thing
65. And it went bbchhh! All over everywhere.

Stanza 15

66. He's like, "Oh no!"
67. Well Kel's like, Kelly goes, "What happened, What happened? What did you do now Mike?"
68. He goes, "I broke the table",
69. She's like "[sigh]", like that.

SUB-STORY 2: MONEY FROM WINDOW FALLING
ON HAND
Stanza 16

70. He just got money from his lawyers
71. Because he slit, he slit his wrists last year,
72. Not on purpose,
73. He did it with, like the window fell down on him,

Stanza 17

74. Well, anyway, it came down and sliced his hand like right um here
75. And has a scar there
76. And um, it was bleeding
77. So they had to rush him to the hospital,
78. It wouldn't stop,
79. He had stitches.

Stanza 18

80. And they said that he could sue,
81. And they got five grand.
82. So they just got it two weeks ago
83. So he just bought her new table.

FRAME
Stanza 19

84. He's okay.
85. He's, he's nice in a caring,
86. He's like really sweet

Sandra organizes her oral text in terms of "the principle of the echo", that is, later parts of the text echo or mirror earlier ones, a key device in oral story-telling in many cultures. This lends—to switch to a visual metaphor—to a "boxes within boxes" shape to her text. Below, in Figure 7.1, the structure of Sandra's oral text is outlined, notating but a few of its most salient echoing features (for some readers, Figure 7.1 may be distracting until they have read the analysis of Sandra's story—feel free to skip it, if that is the case, and come back to it later, if you want):

Sandra's whole oral text is bracketed by a repeated frame: the boyfriend is nice. The main story is composed of two sub-stories. The first ("sub-story 1") is about losses caused by the boyfriend accidentally breaking things. The second ("sub-story 2") is about the boyfriend gaining money because a thing (i.e., a window) has accidentally "broken" him (i.e., injuring his wrists). This "inverse accident" leads to one of the "lost" things being restored (i.e., the table), yet another sort of inversion. And, of course, "restoration" of a "lack/loss" is a classic narrative closing device in oral-based cultures. The first sub-story ("sub-story 1") is itself composed of two stories. The first ("sub-sub-story 1") is about the breaking of the fan; the second ("sub-sub-story 2") is about the breaking of the table.

There are large amounts of parallelism between the two breaking narratives (the fan and the table). Both begin with expository stanzas saying that the boyfriend's actions always go unpunished. These stanzas are followed, in both cases, by "fooling around" involving the boyfriend. Then, in each case, an object falls and makes a noise. The accident leads, in the first case, to the being asked, "What did you do now?" These questions both go unanswered.

The fan story closes with the mother issuing a verbal command to the boyfriend to stop laughing, a command that goes unheeded. The table story

FRAME: S1: Boyfriend is nice

_____

|STORY: Replacing the table

| _____

| |SUB-STORY 1: Breaking things

| | _____

| | |SUB-SUB-STORY 1: Breaking the fan

| | | |

| | | | S2–3:   Exposition: Boyfriend does things, nobody cares

| | | |

| | | | S4:   Mother fooling around with boyfriend leads to:

| | | |

| | | | S6:   Fan falls and makes noise: kkrrhhh

| | | | Boyfriend laughs

| | | |

| | | | S7:   Boyfriend laughs

| | | | Boyfriend makes noise: hahahahah!

| | | |

| | | | S8:   Mother asks: "What are you doing Mike?"

| | | |

| | | | S9:   Mother tells boyfriend not to laugh

| | | | Boyfriend keeps laughing

| | | |_____

| | |

| | | _____

| | |SUB-SUB-STORY 2: Breaking the table

| | | |

| | | | S10–12:   Exposition: Boyfriend does things, doesn't get in trouble

| | | |

| | | | S13:   Boyfriend fooling around with the girls leads to:

| | | |

| | | | S14:   Table falls & makes noise: blopp! bbchhh!

| | | |

| | | | S15:   Kelly asks "What did you do now, Mike?"

| | | | Kelly makes a noise: sigh

| | | |_____

| | |_____

| |

| |

| | _____

| |

| |SUB-STORY 2:   Boyfriend gets money from window falling on his hand

| |_____

|

|END OF STORY: Boyfriend replaces table ("So he just bought her new table")

FRAME: S19: Boyfriend is nice

Figure 7.1 Outline of Sandra's story with some "echoes" noted

closes with the boyfriend's sister issuing no verbal command, but merely an unverbalized sigh. The boyfriend's laughter in the first story is echoed by his sister's sigh in the second.

These two breaking stories are both about "accidents" involving the boyfriend that lead to loss (fan, table). They are followed by a story (sub-story 2) about another accident involving the boyfriend—only this accident is not play, but a serious injury; a person rather than a thing breaks; and the accident leads not to loss, but to gain (money) and restoration (the table). In the fan story, the boyfriend will not heed his mother when she asks him to stop laughing. In the window story, the boyfriend restores the table to the mother without being asked to do so. Such "reversals" and "inversions," are, of course, powerful integrative or connection devices. Additionally, this sort of parallel structuring lends a certain "equivalence logic" to the text. Different stanzas are equated either through direct similarity or reversals, a looser sort of similarity.

One of my interests, as a linguist, in Sandra's story was this: it is now well known that many African-American children, teenagers, and adults can tell extremely well-formed "oral style" stories (which, by no means, implies they are not perfectly literate, as well)—though this style of storytelling is not usually "successful" in school, especially in the early years. These stories share aspects of the style of Western oral-culture "classics" such as biblical stories and Homer's epics (not to mention a great many non-Western oral-culture "classics"), as well as aspects of literature, such as some poetry and the prose of "modernist" writers such as James Joyce and Virginia Woolf. They also incorporate some features unique to African-American culture, as well as features rooted in African cultures.

We know much less—next to nothing—about the "natural occurring" (i.e., non-school-based) narrative abilities of white working-class people, especially children and teenagers. What little has been said is often negative.

Sandra's story encapsulates many of the themes and motifs we have discussed above: disconnection (no direct consequences for boyfriend's acts; table is restored unasked); disavowal of authoritative language as efficacious (the mother's command goes unheeded, her question and the sister's go unanswered; the sister/peer only sighs); a world of laughter, noise, and physical and social action interaction; a world of accidents and play, not facts and knowledge; a world in which what counts is the affect (e.g., laughter) you effect in others.

We can see that the sorts of hypotheses we drew from our study of Sandra's motifs, hypotheses which are illuminated by and draw further support from a study of Sandra's first-person statements (not discussed here), help, in turn, to illuminate the deeper sense of Sandra's narrative. At the same time, our analysis of that narrative gives us further support for the sorts of hypotheses we can draw from Sandra's motifs. What we are gaining here, then, is coverage (ideas inspired by one part of the data extend to and illuminate other parts) and convergence (ideas from new parts of the data continue to support ideas we have identified from other parts of the data). Further, we have begun to support our ideas with a variety of different linguistic details in the data (linguistics).

Ultimately, what we see is that Sandra thematizes an opposition between "authoritative representation" and "sympathetic social interaction" as part and parcel of her "identity work". Since the realm of "authoritative representation" is quite likely to be associated with schools, Sandra's very identity work will (and, in fact, does) work against her affiliation with school, unless the school comes to know, understand, and adapt to her language and identities.

Recommended reading

William Labov and Joshua Waletzky (1967). Narrative Analysis. In J. Helm, Ed., *Essays on the Verbal and Visual Arts*. Seattle, WA: University of Washington Press, pp. 12–44. Reprinted in *Journal of Narrative and Life History* 7: 3–38, 1997.

Ivor Armstrong (I. A.) Richards (1924). *Principles of Literary Criticism*. New Edition, 1926. Routledge Classics Edition, 2001. London: Routledge and Kegan Paul.

8

Tools

8.1 Reverse engineering

One way to understand any designed thing—for example, a bridge, a computer, or a building—is to "reverse engineer" it. By this I mean to take it apart to see how it is designed and built. In the process, we seek to understand the function of each part; how the parts fit and function together; and often how the whole has properties that are more than the sum of its parts.

Much of what we have talked about in this book are tools to take language-in-use apart, to reverse engineer it. Grammar tells us the brute construction of language-in-use, much like the physical parts of a bike or a building. Other tools—the tools of discourse analysis that build on, but go beyond grammar— tell us how these "parts" (choices, patterns, oppositions) function alone, together, and as a system. The tools are essentially **questions** we ask of the data we want to analyze (Fairclough 2003, 2010; Gee 2014a, 2014b).

These are questions we discourse analysts can ask to help us explicate the meaning-making process:

1. **Identity**:
   What identity or identities are being enacted?
2. **Activity (practice):**
   What activity or activities are being carried out?
3. **Social language:**
   What social language or social languages are being used?
4. **Recipient design:**
   How has the language been designed to invite or guide recipients to interpret and respond in certain ways?

5. **Situational meaning:**
   What situational meanings are being communicated?

6. **Connections:**
   How is the speaker or writer expressing what he or she sees as connected (and how) and not connected (disconnected)? (Cohesion is one, but not the only, grammatical way in which connections are signaled.)

7. **Discourse:**
   How is language and "other stuff" being used in dynamic interaction? What Discourses are at work and in what ways?

8. **Significance:**
   How is the speaker or writer indicating what is significant or important and what is less so or not at all?

9. **Social relationships:**
   What sorts of social relationships is the speaker or writer trying to create, sustain, support, change, or tear apart?

10. **Politics:**
    How does the speaker or writer construe, support, or advocate how "social goods" are or should be distributed? By "social goods" I mean anything a society or a Discourse takes as a good, valuable, or necessary thing to have.

11. **Perspectives**
    What perspectives or viewpoints is the speaker or writer expressing?

12. **Frameworks**
    See Chapter 9.

These tools/questions are part of the tool kit of discourse analysts. But it is important to see that they are also part of the tool kit of any speaker or writer. Speakers and writers must ask themselves these questions and answer them in order to use grammar to design what they want to say and do with language. They ask themselves these questions in a form like: "How should I use language here and how to indicate to others what I take to be significant and important and what I take to be not as significant or important?"

Speakers most often ask these questions unconsciously and in real time, as they speak to and respond to others. Writers often, but not always, take more time and conscious thought to deal with these questions. Speakers and writers use these questions to plan what they want to say and do with language, while discourse analysts use them (overtly and consciously) to understand what speakers and writers are trying to say and do and what the consequences may be.

Note that we can take the questions in any order. Some orders work better or worse for different data. I often put identity and Discourses together since they are opposite sides of the same coin: identity is a person enacting a Discourse and Discourse is a historical process and set of ways with words, deeds, and things that allow people to enact socially recognizable identities. So, identity throws light on a person in action spinning Discourses in his or her own way and Discourse throws light on how larger historical, social, cultural, institutional, and political forces speak and act through us.

I will skip covering connections further here, since this tool/question was amply discussed in Chapter 7. In Chapter 9, we will discuss Frameworks (Tool 12).

8.2 Grammar, social languages, choices, and perspectives

We have seen that grammar sets up choices. These choices are determined not just by the general grammar of English, but also by the specific social language(s) being used. So, we must always ask what social language or set of them is at play and what sorts of grammatical choices were made that could have been made differently. The social language in which the passage below is written is obvious to anyone who knows the activities and Discourse in which it plays a role (see: Gee 2012):

1. Mitigation from armor class is the only non-linearly scaling stat (that is, each percent of mitigation granted by Armor Class requires more than the point before it).

This is a sentence from a "theory crafting" site where *World of Warcraft* (a massive, multiplayer video game) players analyze the underlying statistics and rules of the game. If you wanted to study this social language, you would have to understand what it does, how it functions, why people do it, and what they get from it, in the Discourses of gaming, multiplayer games, or theory-crafting, depending upon what level you were looking at (remember, there are Discourses within Discourses within Discourses, like neighborhoods within cities within states).

Not all social languages are as clear and unmixed as the example above. In this regard, consider this sentence from page 65 of Michael Eric Dyson's book, *Tears We Cannot Stop: A Sermon to White America* (2017):

> Most black folk can't help but notice what many whites rarely wish, or are compelled, to see: you embrace history as your faithful flame when she kisses you, and yet you spurn her as a cheating mate when she nods or winks at others.

In this part of his book, Dyson is talking about how the historical contributions of white people are predominant in American history books, but the contributions of others—Native Americans, brown people, and black people—are often left out. He is saying that white people tend to like history books only when whites are front and center and not when other sorts of American people are.

What sort of social language is this text is written? What sorts of grammatical choices has Dyson made (and why) that he could have made otherwise?

As to the social language, note how poetic the language of this passage is, even though it is prose:

> Most black folk can't help but notice what many whites rarely wish, or are compelled, to see: you embrace history as your faithful flame when she kisses you, and yet you spurn her as a cheating mate when she nods or winks at others.

This passage is organized around lexical and grammatical parallelism and opposition. Note:

Most blacks—many whites
Can't help—rarely wish
Can't help—are compelled
Notice—see—winks
You embrace—you spurn
Faithful flames—cheating mate
She kisses you—she nods or winks at others

Dyson is a well-known academic, a public intellectual, an African-American, and a Baptist minister. He tells us his book is a sermon to white America. His book is a mixture of several different social languages: the language of sermons, the language of certain sorts of black churches, poetic prose, academic language, and the less academic, but still formal, vernacular of an author writing for a larger (not just academic) public. These different social languages interweave and crisscross in Dyson's book. The passage above highlights poetic prose, though it is influenced by the other strands of social languages in the book.

Now, let's consider the grammatical choices Dyson made. Below I reprint Dyson's passage and a version I wrote making different choices:

1. Most black folk can't help but notice what many whites rarely wish, or are compelled, to see: you embrace history as your faithful flame when she kisses you, and yet you spurn her as a cheating mate when she nods or winks at others.
2. Most black people, but few white ones, notice that many whites enjoy reading history books only when these books focus on white people's contributions to history, but not when they focus on non-whites and their contributions.

In my version (2), the poetry is gone and we have a rather bare claim. The whole concept of whites in love with white history (and, thus, themselves) is gone. The sexual metaphors are gone: faithful flame, kisses, spurn, cheating mate, wink, and nod. Why might Dyson have made the choices he did? One reason may well be that he wants to portray reading history as a love of self—as an affirmation of one's favored identity—for American whites, not as a rational act of fact-seeking or seeking to learn uncomfortable truths. Historical texts are seen as a mirror into which the white reader stares at his or her own reflection with love or admiration. The poetry and metaphors make meanings that go beyond bare prosaic facts about reading demographics.

(1) and (2) say similar things. Both could be true. Nonetheless, even if they are, they are different perspectives (ways to look at) history reading on the part of white and blacks.

8.3 Recipient design

Dyson's book is a dramatic example of recipient design, making the complexity of the concept clear indeed. His book is sub-titled "A Sermon to White America". Dyson also calls the book a "jeremiad, an extended lamentation about the woes we face" (named after the Old Testament prophet Jeremiah).

As an individual person ("Jim") with my own history, I am not very familiar with Baptist sermons, only Catholic ones (I was raised as, and long was, a devoted Catholic). I am, however, very familiar with the Old

Testament and Jeremiah. From general cultural knowledge, and from media, I assume a Baptist sermon involves a minister addressing the congregation as sinners in need of salvation. I know Jeremiah's jeremiads were complaints to God, messages of woe to the Jewish people, and a forceful call for the people to clean up their act or face devastation. I also know Dyson is an academic and I know some of his other work. I know he is not a religious fanatic; that he is well aware of how vexed religion has, at times, been in the world, as people kill other people in the name of God; and he certainly sees both religion and secular citizenship as demanding mercy and justice.

Consider, again, the passage we dealt with above:

1. Most black folk can't help but notice what many whites rarely wish, or are compelled, to see: you embrace history as your faithful flame when she kisses you, and yet you spurn her as a cheating mate when she nods or winks at others.

Now, it just so happens that I have read a good many historical books, memoirs, and political and social books by and about African-Americans and some, but less, about Native-Americans. One of my favorite history books is Howard Zinn's masterful *A People's History of the United States* (1980), which is about the contributions of non-whites to US history. I have always loved James Loewen's *Lies My History Teacher Told Me* (1995), a book which makes it clear that American history textbooks are full of inaccuracies and lies.

So, for all sorts of reasons, including my religious past, my reading, and my own views about history, the "you" in Dyson's passage above cannot be addressing "Jim" directly or personally (how could he, he cannot know all his readers). So, what do I do if I want to be a compliant reader and accept the reader position or reader identity Dyson is inviting me to take up?

In a sermon addressing sinners (and this was true of Catholics, as well) no one gets off claiming that they themselves are not sinners, that only other people are. Many Christian sects teach that all humans are frail and sinners and if the minister is talking at the moment about someone else's sin, you are meant to meditate on your own until he or she gets around to it.

Furthermore, both on religious terms and secular ones, we humans can bear moral responsibility for bad things even if we were not direct agents in making them happen. There are "sins" of omission (what you did not do, but should have) and there are ways some people (e.g., white people and rich people) have often benefited from injustices visited on others and, thus, they may well need to think about what to "give back" (return to the person who lost it, when they have found it).

Furthermore, there is something specific to my Catholic background that I can call on to put myself in the sort of reader position Dyson's text asks me to take up. Catholics believe in a thing called an "examination of conscience", often used to prepare for confession. In an examination of conscience, the sinner seeks to ferret out all his or her sins, no matter how forgotten, hidden, or subject to self-denial they may be. The examination of conscience is preparation for forgiveness, so, in a deep sense, the Catholic has nothing to lose by "coming clean".

What we can see here is that I can, if I want, draw on aspects of my own personal background, on parts of my cultural knowledge, and on Dyson's text (and how he has written/designed it) to construct a way to read that (I think) takes up something like the reader position/identity Dyson is trying to design for me and other readers. Other readers will have to do this act of construction differently, since they have different backgrounds, cultural knowledge, and ways of reading texts. Taking up recipient design to be a compliant reader is an act of choice, construction, understanding, interpretation, and negotiation, even with oneself. It is a contract that the speaker or author offers the listener or reader, one that can be negotiated, but not entirely abrogated, if we seek understanding.

Why, though, be a compliant—rather than a resistant—reader? There are two reasons: one is that Dyson asks you, like any good author does, to trust him and hope that if you take up the reader position he offers you, you will learn something and come away with some good things. The other reason—one connected to the nature of discourse analysis—is that even if we want to resist or criticize Dyson we cannot really do this in a fair, just, and meaningful way if we have not actually tried to understand him and accept, for the nonce at least, his textual invitations.

There are, of course, some readers—as Dyson very well knows—who will, even at the start, resist him and refuse to be a compliant reader. Indeed, some readers will find his text insulting or otherwise decry it. It is also interesting to think about how the way Dyson constructs a reader position for whites, but constructs a quite different one for black people who read his book (they are, in a sense, overhearers, perhaps listening to the sins of others, while quietly also meditating on their own). Speakers and writers make meaning by making choices. Listeners and readers have choices to make, too.

Recipient design, in speech or writing, is active design work intended to guide the listener or reader to read and respond in certain ways. In the best of cases, the listener or reader listens or reads not just as a private self, but as a joint venture of self, author, and words, and other grammatical choices. In the act, we may gain fuel to become something new and to think new thoughts and do new things. Of course, like all powerful tools, recipient design can be an invitation for good or for evil. So, indeed, sometimes we do have to resist with all our might. But we do often, too, have to be careful not to confuse something that makes us uncomfortable with something that is wrong or bad.

8.4 Situational meanings

We have seen that words and phrases have core meanings (semantics) based on the mental lexicon that is part of the grammar of our language. But these core meanings—which basically set the meaning potential of words—must be situated within, adapted to, and nuanced for specific contexts of use. Indeed, being able to do this is what demonstrates a person's interactional competence within specific social settings and Discourses. If we do know what context something was said within, we can know basic meanings but still be at a loss for what things actually mean. Take, for example, the conversation below:

Bead: Are you really dead
Allele: Yes, did you get the heart?
Bead: I got the heart—another guy was helping
Allele: Good
Bead: I am standing over your body mourning
Allele: I died for you
Bead: So touching
Allele: It's a long way back
Bead: I know—I've done it

Here it is clear that words like "dead", "body", "died", and "long way back" have contextually specific meanings that go beyond their core meanings (e.g., the core meaning of "dead" is "a formerly animate being that is no longer living"). If you do not know the context here, these lines sound like something from a postmodern play. What we have here are two brothers (in real life) talking to each other as characters in a massive multiplayer video game (*World of Warcraft*). In such games, avatars (the "surrogate body" a player has in the game) can die but still come back to life, though their "spirit" must walk back to where its body died. The two players were trying to complete a quest in the game to find a heart buried in the ground. They were attacked by monsters and Allele died fighting them off, as did another player who just happened to be there and decided to help. With their help, Bead was able to defeat the monsters, stay alive, and get the heart.

Consider this example from a video game manual:

> Your internal nano-processors keep a very detailed record of your condition, equipment and recent history. You can access this data at any time during play by hitting F1 to get to the Inventory screen or F2 to get to the Goals/Notes screen.

Gamers—familiar with the context of gaming—will realize that "your" in the first sentence refers to something different than does "you" in the second sentence. "Your" in the first sentence means the player's avatar (in-game character). The player as a real person has no nano-processors. The "you" in the second sentence means the player, the real person. The game character cannot push on the computer's buttons, only the player can. By the way, it is part of gamer Discourse that gamers regularly and often use "I" for their character (as in "I died"), thereby melding their real-world self with their in-game avatar self.

In Michael Eric Dyson's passage we looked at above, what is the situational meaning of "black folk"? "Black" here does not mean color *per se*. It means primarily African-Americans. It includes African-Americans who are not close to being black in color, but various shades of brown. Furthermore, there are lots of brown or black people in the USA, and in the world, that are not African-Americans. Does "black" include Africans who happen in live in the USA, but are not African-American? I assume Dyson means by "black" all people in America connected to Africa that have been victims of racism. But my point is that the reader must assume something to give the word a specific and useful meaning in the text.

But what does "folk" add to this? The word "folk" here is an informal vernacular way to talk about a group of people in a friendly way ("folks like us", "hey, folks, it's time for dinner"). But "folk" can also mean "connected to traditional or common culture" ("folk music", "folk dancing", "folk tale"). This use of the word took on unfortunate connotations in Germany, where the German word for "folk" ("volk") was used by the Nazis to mean the German nation or race, as in *Ein Volk, ein Reich, ein Führer* ("One nation or race, one empire, one leader"). Dyson surely does not intend "folk" to carry this latter meaning in his text, though his use of "folk" in the singular (meant here just to be vernacular) might trigger it for some readers more than the term "black folks" would have.

Think about how much one needs to know culturally about race in the USA to make contextual sense of "black folks" and "whites" in Dyson's text. We rarely stop to think much about this wealth of culturally specific knowledge that allows us to make sense of what words mean in different contexts of use.

In any consideration of language-in-use both the people communicating and discourse analysts must be aware of what the context is and how this affects the situational meaning of words and phrases. They often also must be aware of what Discourses are at play and how they are shaping how language is being used both in that context and to construe and construct that context at the same time.

Contextualization cues (which we discussed in Section 6.8)—when they are present—are a way speakers signal how they want listeners to situate their meanings in context, a context that their contextualization cues are helping the listener to construe in a certain way.

8.5 Actions and activities

Any time we talk or write we are trying to do something. We are trying to inform, persuade, encourage, request, deny, praise, bond, or many other things. Talking and writing are always forms of acting. Earlier I said that there is a difference between actions and activities (or what some scholars call "practices"). When a pitcher in a baseball game throws the ball towards home plate from the pitcher's mound, that is an action. But pitching is also an activity that is done in similar (but not identical) ways repeatedly and is regulated (in terms of how, where, when, and why it is done) by groups and institutions, namely, baseball leagues and the sport of baseball (Hacking 1999).

Activities (practices) are conventional ways that people with certain identities have developed to get their "work" done, to function to do what they are interested in, such as birding, doing physics, gaming, gardening, lawyering, engaging in gang activities, teaching in school, and so forth.

So, for any language-in-use data, we want to ask what actions are being carried out, but also what activities or practices—associated with what identities or Discourses—are being carried out as well. We want to know that the pitcher threw a curve ball (an action) and that he is pitching in big league baseball (an activity).

Returning to Dyson's passage, reprinted below, what is he doing in terms of actions and activities:

> Most black folk can't help but notice what many whites rarely wish, or are compelled, to see: you embrace history as your faithful flame when she kisses you, and yet you spurn her as a cheating mate when she nods or winks at others.

At the level of actions enacted by language, Dyson here is making a claim (informing) and he is also making an accusation of hypocrisy, "bad faith", or inconsistency, whatever we want to call it. Both the information and the accusation are not "pleasant" for the intended reader ("you"), namely white people in their identity as people privileged by "whiteness". Language actions like accusation are tricky, indeed. They can lead to anger, rejection, and, thus, here a failure to read the book.

What are some of the activities (practices) Dyson is engaging in? Well, one activity is that he is writing as an academic public intellectual. Such books usually assert facts and arguments in a fairly dispassionate way. They are like public lectures. Dyson is aware that in this case, however, such facts and arguments might well cause readers, as an emotional response, to quit reading early on in his book. Dyson's own strong feelings, and sometimes quite negative personal experiences as a black man in a white world—and white readers' own strong (but varied) emotions in regard to race—would seem to make this a very hard book to write as a typical academic public intellectual sort of book.

Therefore, Dyson chooses to write his book with lots of the sorts of content (facts and arguments) that appear in an academic book or one written by a public intellectual, but in the form or style of a sermon rather than a lecture. A sermon is a very different activity (practice) than a lecture. Sermons allow for emotion, accusations of sinning, examination of conscience, penance, and hopes for forgiveness and even a better world. The author of a sermon is channeling a moral voice, not speaking as a professional "expert".

However, Dyson is not "really" giving a sermon. He is not in church. He is using "his God" to get readers not to show allegiance to his God (as a minister in church would do), but to show allegiance to whatever deeper moral forces move them.

Thus, Dyson has combined two Discourses (academic public intellectual and minister). In the act, he has created something new for most of his readers, namely a sermon that is public and not encased in a specific church. Such things were not, in fact, rare in the past. Puritan divines in New England, for example, often published sermons as public messages for a wide reading public. Dyson is harkening back to this tradition by imagining a future in which we all, black and white, would share a common faith in ourselves as all together better Americans and humans.

Activities are often mundane and somewhat ritualized, as when we chat about the weather, report for jury duty, write an editorial or a letter to the editor of a newspaper, send a text message to friends, give a report at work, or ask for forgiveness in confession. But activities can be blended, dynamic, and innovative—as is Dyson's sermon—as long as there is still enough conventional common ground left for readers or listeners to key into what is going on.

8.6 Perspective design

I have repeatedly said in this book that grammar gives us choices and that the choices we make express perspectives on the world, not transparent, unvarnished truth. The language design tools we discussed in the last chapter help us analysts get at perspectives by showing us how they were expressed in a specific situation. The perspective design tools we will discuss here help us to analyze this expression—this "way with words"—to understand the perspective the speaker is trying to express.

Grammar gives speakers a tool kit of choices. These choices create patterns, oppositions, foregrounded and backgrounded information, connections and disconnections, ways of naming things, expressions of emotion, and links to the world that guide listeners and discourse analysts as to what to pay attention to and how to pay attention to it. Just in the same way good painters use design (with paint) to direct and guide the viewer's eye and reaction to their painting, so, too, speakers use design (with grammar) as a way to direct and guide the listener's attention and interpretations.

We can get at the perspectives (viewpoints) people are taking by asking all the questions (using all the tools) we have listed in this chapter. They are all relevant since the goal of making grammatical choices is to express a perspective. However, the following tools/questions (and connections) are particularly salient for uncovering a speaker's or writer's perspective.

8.7 Significance

Some things in the world are of a great importance to almost any human, things like life and death. But a great many other things are more important to some people than to others. Different people weigh the importance of things differently and the same people can weigh their importance differently in different situations. The significance tool/question asks how a speaker or writer is making certain things important or foregrounded and other things less important or backgrounded.

Here is something Dyson tells us very early in his book:

> Although I am a scholar, a cultural and political critic, and a social activist, I am, before, and above anything else, an ordained Baptist minister. Please don't hold that against me, although I'll understand if you do. I know that religion has a bad rap. We believers deserve a lot of the criticism that we receive. (Dyson, 2017: p. 4)

Here Dyson tells us that of all his identities relevant to the book, his identity as an ordained Baptist minister is most important. At the same time, he acknowledges the significance of the bad reputation religion has to some secular people and he takes this criticism seriously, something many other religious people downplay (and this is one of many signs in the book that Dyson is a rather "secularist" version of a Baptist minister).

By overtly mentioning "ordained" he signals that being ordained is important and implies, but does not say, there are unordained Baptist ministers. A Catholic priest would probably not write "I am an ordained Catholic priest" because all Catholic priests are, by definition, ordained by a bishop. So, for me as a reader, a person who knows more about Catholicism than Baptists, Dyson's stress on the significance of being ordained implies to me that there are, among Baptists, controversies here. So, of course, I looked it up on the internet and found things like this:

> In most denominations, ordination refers to the process of being officially recognized and established by an ecclesiastical authority like an elder, a bishop, or a cardinal to be a minister. Given the independent nature of most baptist churches, it's unclear who is doing the ordination and what it means.
>
> … ordination is done by each local congregation, and each congregation decides for itself what the requirements and prerequisites are, and may or

may not consult other churches before doing so. Some don't even require ordination of its pastors.

(http://christianity.stackexchange.com/questions/45931/what-do-baptists-mean-when-they-refer-to-an-ordained-baptist-minister)

I am not concerned with the accuracy of this citation from the internet, just with the fact that Dyson's use of the word "ordained" has led me to see that the word and concept play a different role—and is significant in a different way—than the word and concept is in some other sects such as Catholicism.

8.8 Social relations

Dyson designs his writing to construct several different social relationships with his readers. These include black and white, minister and sinner, academic and pupil, and fellow citizen to fellow citizen. In addition, Dyson's writing, especially his strategic and changing use of "you" and "we" throughout the text, takes a perspective on how Americans are socially related; how they socially interact with each other; and how they could change those relationships.

We saw above that Dyson's passage on history is organized around oppositions. Indeed, one perspective that runs across a good deal of Dyson's writing in his book is that some social oppositions can trap us and we can only be "saved" when we destroy them.

The leading opposition in his book is, of course, "black–white". Dyson is aware that black and white as races are a social construction with no real tie to biology, but with real and sometimes dire consequences, especially for black people, but not only for black people. As long as this opposition holds, all of us are not really free to be and see each other as individuals. We become categories or symbols, not real flesh and blood people.

> We are two historical forces meeting, and the velocity of that history is so strong that it can break the bonds of individual love. We are no longer two people asking each other to be understood. Instead, we are two symbols in a 400-year-old battle of guilt and innocence. (Dyson, 2017: p. 102)

Note the use of "we" here, compared to the many uses of "you" earlier in the text. Ironically, this "we" unites us at the very point Dyson makes the divide most stark (a four-hundred-year-old battle, acted out on bodies and minds, between two opposing symbols). Nonetheless, this "we" holds out a ray of hope. At the end of his book, Dyson suggests that if we finally do the work to heal and destroy the black–white opposition, we will we all be brought together as a colorful myriad of diverse people who are different in many ways, but who share a good many things, including being what, for better or worse, we have always been, fellow Americans, those who together made America:

> Oh Lord, black folk are everything; we are every possibility of American, even human, identity made real. That means we are everywhere, just like our white brothers and sisters. (Dyson, 2017: p. 228)

8.9 Politics

By "politics" I do not mean political parties and elections. I mean how speakers and writers express what they take to be social goods and how they are, or should be, distributed, shared, contested, and fought over. A social good is anything some group of people take as valuable, good, wanted, or necessary to have. Some social goods are society wide: nearly every human being considers respect and freedom to be social goods. There are also social goods that only some groups value, for example, citations for an academic or inclusion in a guild for some gamers.

Dyson, of course, is dealing with the fact that many white people in the USA have spoken and written, and continue to speak and write— sometimes overtly and sometimes subtly—as if African-Americans are not as smart, adept, American, or even as human as white people. These are, of course, all social goods to both black and white Americans. So, when we express perspectives on these issues, we are, in my terms, engaged in "politics" (the distribution of social goods).

Dyson's use of "ordained" signals that this is something he considers a social good and that he has. And, he implies, perhaps, that that social good is contestable in various ways, as would seem to be the case if my internet citation above is accurate.

Reconsider the quote from Dyson below:

> We are two historical forces meeting, and the velocity of that history is so strong that it can break the bonds of individual love. We are no longer two people asking each other to be understood. Instead, we are two symbols in a 400-year-old battle of guilt and innocence.

Here, Dyson treats love and being understood as two social goods that all people who are fellow Americans want, need, and have a right to. In turn, these social goods cannot be properly distributed—for the good of all—until we stop treating each other as symbols and not people. Note, too, that 400-year-old battle is a fight over a social ill (guilt) and a social good (innocence). Each party in this longer running battle apportions and accepts guilt and innocence differently.

8.10 Identities and discourses

So, let's now return to identities and Discourses. Dyson is balancing several different identities, connected to different Discourses. These include:

Academic
Public intellectual
African–American male of a certain sort
Baptist minister
Father in an upper-middle-class family

Discourses are ways to enact socially meaningful identities, using language and "other stuff" such as ways of dressing, acting, interacting, valuing, believing, and using various sorts of objects, tools, and technologies, often in specific sorts of places and sometimes at specific times. Being a Baptist minister is different than being a Catholic priest, and these are different from being an academic. But one person can be all three at different times and places and all three identities can influence each other at any one time and place.

Discourses use certain sorts of social languages, they situate meanings in certain ways, and they carry out certain sorts of characteristic actions and activities. People within a given Discourse address each other (recipiently design what they say or write) in certain characteristic ways and they address people in other Discourses in certain characteristic ways, as well.

Writers must rely on language more than speakers. When we speak face-to-face, lots of non-language stuff is readily available for meaning making: how we dress; where we are speaking; what objects or tools we are using while speaking and interacting; and the whole environment around us, as well as any shared history of interactions.

Dyson is lecturing, but without a lecture hall. He is preaching, but without a pulpit or a church. He is engaged with public media (a book he wants to be read widely by the public), but he is not now on TV where we can see and hear him. He has no idea what he shares with specific readers of his book, though he can make some rather general assumptions. When he wants to express his "creds" (credibility) as an African-American man, a minister, a media figure, or an academic, we cannot see him "talk the talk and walk the walk", we can only see him "write the writing". This gives writing great potential for play with identities, allows things to be said that could not be said otherwise, but it also makes writing a difficult (and at times a lonely) task, indeed, since it is not embedded in a personal interaction.

In the USA, blacks and whites both belong to the Discourse of "being American". They all know how to enact forms of recognizable American-ness. White Americans (no matter who they are) have no trouble recognizing black Americans as Americans and not foreigners, Africans, or tourists. Black Americans (no matter who they are) can readily tell a white American from a foreign white person, even if they both speak English. White Americans can tell a middle-class black person from a lower-socioeconomic black person and blacks can do the same for whites. Black and white Americans share immense common knowledge and they all know various ways to enact, react to, and recognize, not race in general, but race in America. At the same time, there are different ways to be black or white in America, different types of black and white people, and there are many "kinds of people" (Discourses) which include both black and white people.

Discourses need not be harmonious. They often contain people who also have other identities—people who belong to other Discourses—that might be in conflict. Gamers, doctors, soldiers, academics, and politicians all have other identities in terms of which they can—and sometimes do—have conflicts with each other. Nonetheless, they know how to be "the same thing", when they have to be or want to be, otherwise their shared Discourse dies. Indeed, every Discourse, to survive, must have ways to mitigate the conflicts outside identities can have within the Discourse.

I have chosen Michael Eric Dyson's book to use as an example text for discourse analysis because it is bound to be a contentious text in today's world. There will be white readers (and maybe even some black readers) who will be insulted and, perhaps, even angered by the book. One of the most serious problems we face today, in the age of the internet, social media, and ideological polarization, is that people try less and less to discuss contentious issues with each other and simply disdain or dismiss people with whom they disagree. This has led to a deeply divided world in which people have a great deal of trouble working together to solve problems and not working against each other to make problems worse. It is to this issue we turn in our final chapter.

References

Dyson, M. E. (2017). *Tears We Cannot Stop: A Sermon to White America*. New York: St. Martin's Press.

Fairclough, N. (2003). *Analyzing Discourse: Textual Analysis for Social Research*. London: Routledge.

Fairclough, N. (2010). *Critical Discourse Analysis: The Critical Study of Language*. Second Edition. London: Longman.

Gee, J. P. (2012). The Old and the New in the New Digital Literacies. *The Educational Forum* 76.4: 418–420.

Gee, J. P. (2014a). *An Introduction to Discourse Analysis: Theory and Method*. Fourth Edition. London: Routledge.

Gee, J. P. (2014b). *How to Do Discourse Analysis: A Toolkit*. Second Edition. London: Routledge.

Hacking, I. (1999). *The Social Construction of What?* Cambridge, MA: Harvard University Press.

Loewen, H. (1995). *Lies My History Teacher Told Me: Everything Your American History Textbook Got Wrong*. New York: The New Press.

Zinn, H. (1980). *A People's History of the United States*. New York: Harper-Collins.

9 Perspectives, frameworks, and conversations

9.1 Context

Context is crucial to understanding language-in-use and for doing discourse analysis (Schegloff 1997; Silverstein 1992; Tracy 2010; van Dijk 2008). When we speak, rarely can we say all that we mean. Spelling everything out in words explicitly would take far too long. Speakers rely on listeners to use the context in which things are said to fill in meanings that are left unsaid, but assumed to be inferable from context. Even a simple utterance like, "The paper is on the table", requires that the hearer infer from context which paper and which table is meant.

Context includes the physical setting in which communication takes place; the bodies, eye gaze, gestures, and movements of those present; what has previously been said and done by those involved in the communication; and any shared personal, social, and cultural knowledge.

Context in writing is obviously different than context in speech, because writer and reader are not face to face, physically encountering each other. Gesture and eye gaze do not play a role, for example. But the previous text before the current statement being read, and any shared knowledge (including the history of genres and texts), are still both parts of the context for writing.

When we think about how context works, we quickly face an important property of language, a property I will call "reflexivity". This is a rather "magical" property. We can see this property clearly by considering even so simple an exchange as: "How ya doin'? Fine", between two colleagues in an office corridor. Why do they use *these* words in *this* context? *Because* they take the context they are in to be a brief and mundane encounter between fellow workers at work, and these are "appropriate" words to use in such a situation. But why do they take the context to be *thus*? In part, *because* they are using just such words and related behaviors. Had the exchange opened with "What's *your* problem, buddy?" the context would have been construed quite differently, perhaps in terms of former hostilities or of a kidding relationship.

Here we face, then, a chicken-and-egg question: which comes first? The context or the language? This question reflects an important *reciprocity* between language and context: language simultaneously *reflects* context (what is out there in the world) and *constructs* (*construes*) it to be a certain way. While "reciprocity" would be a good term for this property of language, the more commonly used term is "reflexivity" (language and context are like two mirrors facing each other and constantly and endlessly reflecting their own images back and forth between each other).

Language-in-use always simultaneously reflects and constructs the context in which it is used. Certain aspects of the context (for example, that I am talking to a friend) are out there in the world, apart from my talk, and, at the same time, are produced (or reproduced) by my talk (for example, if I talk to my friend as a friend in a friendly way, then I make or mark the relationship between us as one of friendship). A person is a friend of mine even when I am not talking to that person, but he or she would soon cease to be a friend if I did not talk to and treat them as a friend in actual performances.

Discourse analysts must investigate how what is being said is both reflecting the context in which it is said and helping to create (construe that context in a certain way at one and the same time). Context is a dynamic concept and what counts as context changes as people interact. So far in this book, I have often used the words "context" and "situation" interchangeably. The word "situation" is a good one when we want to capture the way in which context is simultaneously "there"; what we make of (how we construe) what is "there"; and what our words (and actions, interactions, emotions, and ways with objects, tools, and technologies as we talk) put "there" in a meaningful way.

Recommended reading

Alessandro Duranti and Charles Goodwin, Eds. (1992). *Rethinking Context: Language as an Interactive Phenomenon.* Cambridge: Cambridge University Press.

9.2 The frame problem

Context raises a big problem both for hearers and discourse analysts. The problem is that context is too big. Any aspect of context can affect the meaning of what is said. Context, however, is indefinitely large, ranging from local matters such as the positioning of bodies and eye gaze, through people's beliefs, to historical, institutional, and cultural settings. No matter how much of the context we have considered in interpreting the full meaning of an utterance, there is always the possibility of considering other and additional aspects of the context, and these new considerations may change how we interpret what is said.

Where do we cut off consideration of context? How do we make judgments about what aspects of the context are relevant to what the speaker wants to mean? How can we be sure any interpretation is "right," if considering further aspects of the context might well change that interpretation? This problem is sometimes referred to as the **frame problem** (Mercer & Sperber 2017; Sperber & Wilson 1986, 1996).

Let me give an example of a situation where how much of the context we consider relevant changes how we interpret an utterance. Take a claim like "Many children die in Africa before they are five years old because they get infectious diseases like malaria". What is the appropriate amount of context within which to assess this claim? We could consider just medical facts, a narrow context. And in such context the claim seems unexceptional. However, consider the wider context described below (see also Lewontin 1991):

Malaria, an infectious disease, is one of the most severe public health problems worldwide. It is a leading cause of death and disease in many developing countries, where young children and pregnant women are the groups most affected. Worldwide, one death in three is from an infectious or communicable disease. However, almost all these deaths occur in the non-industrialized world. Health inequality affects not just how people live, but often dictates how and at what age they die. (see: http://tinaturner0020.blogspot.com/2012/12/chapter-9-deviance-and-control.html and http://www.thirdworldtraveler.com/Health/Cause_Death_Inequality.html)

This wider context (frame) would seem to say that so many children in Africa die early not because of infectious diseases, but because of poverty and economic underdevelopment. While this widening of the context does not necessarily nullify or undermine the explanatory dimension or truth of the original claim, it does allow us to see that the original claim can—or, perhaps, even should—be embedded in a further set of larger claims: many children die in Africa before they are five years old because they get infectious diseases like malaria, and many children in Africa get infectious diseases like malaria before they are five years old because of poverty and economic underdevelopment. And this larger explanatory context can no doubt itself be embedded in a larger one (capitalism, etc.). Widening the context here also makes us realize there are several senses of "because" and number of "causes" in different senses of the word.

The frame problem (how small or big a frame to put around what counts as relevant in the context) is both a problem and a tool. It is a problem because our discourse analytic interpretations (just like people's everyday interpretations of language) are always vulnerable to change as we narrow or widen the context within which we interpret a piece of language. It is a tool because we can use it—by widening the context—to see what information and values are being left unsaid or effaced in a piece of language.

The frame problem, of course, raises problems about validity for discourse analysis. We cannot argue an analysis is valid unless we keep widening the frame (the elements of context that count as relevant) in which we consider a piece of language until the widening appears to make no difference to our interpretation. At that point, we can stop and make our claims (open, of course, to later falsification as in all empirical work). Even then, we may discover that a wider frame raises questions about why someone has framed their utterances in a narrower way. Is it just because the wider frame is truly irrelevant or is there a deep, more meaningful, choice being made?

Framing shows how context is relevant to the perspective a speaker or writer is taking. When we ignore or include the context of poverty in talking about infectious diseases, this may well indicate something important about our perspective on what we are talking about.

9.3 Perspectives

We use grammar to express perspectives on the world (MacWhinney 2000, 2005; Rommetveit 1974, 1980). Two people can make the "same" claim and both speak the truth and yet express that truth from a different point of view. Consider again the two passages on *Heliconius* butterflies we dealt with earlier, one from a science journal and one from a popular science magazine, written by the same scientist (Myers 1990):

> Experiments show that *Heliconius* butterflies are less likely to oviposit on host plants that possess eggs or egg-like structures. These egg-mimics are an unambiguous example of a plant trait evolved in response to a host-restricted group of insect herbivores. (Professional journal)

> *Heliconius* butterflies lay their eggs on *Passiflora* vines. In defense the vines seem to have evolved fake eggs that make it look to the butterflies as if eggs have already been laid on them. (Popular science)

Both passages are about the same "facts". As far as I know, both are true. But the first offers a theoretical perspective, a view from a theory (coevolution), and the second offers a story-based perspective with the butterflies and vines as actors in the story. These are two different ways of looking at the same part of the world. The author (the editors, as well, especially in the case of the popular science version) has made different grammatical choices in each case, ones that express different perspectives.

As another example of perspective taking, consider the remark below from a story told by a middle school white girl about her boyfriend (see Chapter 8):

He smokes /
His mom don't care or nothin //
He smokes weed and everything and nobody cares //
Cos they can't stop him /
He's gonna do it any way //
Like on house arrest he went out anyway //

This girl expresses a perspective here, and elsewhere in her story, that sees adults and adult authority as powerless. She always expresses a perspective on her boyfriend in which his "willfulness" is viewed, if not exactly as an admirable trait, then at least not a bad thing, certainly not a reason not to have him as a boyfriend. In the research from which these data comes, we came to see this perspective as a shared class-based viewpoint. This girl and her fellow lower-class peers saw many (not all) adults as ineffective and uncaring, for the most part, while upper-class teens in this research saw nearly all adults as caring, trustworthy, and in authority.

The perspectives we take are often connected to our social and cultural backgrounds and the Discourses from which we are speaking and acting in a given situation. The scientist is in one case writing as a fellow scientist to other scientists and in the other is writing as a scientist to educated "lay people". The girl is speaking as a lower-class white girl from the poorer part of a post-industrial economically challenged town.

The perspectives we take are situational and social. For example (Harkness, Super, & Keefer 1992), some parents, confronted by a demanding two-year-old who angrily refuses to go to bed, talk as if the child's behavior is a sign of growth towards autonomy because they accept a perspective on children and child-raising like this: children are born dependent on their parents and then they gradually grow towards individual autonomy or independence. On their way to autonomy, they act out, demanding independence, when they may not yet be ready for it, but this is still a sign of development and growth.

Other parents confronted by the same behavior talk as if the child's behavior is a sign of the child's willfulness, because they accept a perspective on children like this: children are born selfish and need to be taught to think of others and to collaborate with the family rather than demand their own way. It is, perhaps, not surprising that this perspective is more common among working-class families where mutual support among family and friends is important. The former perspective is more common among middle and upper-middle-class families with many more financial resources, where people are expected to grow into adults who have the resources to go it on their own.

Such perspectives are not "right" or "wrong". For example, children are, of course, born dependent on their parents. But, are children primarily inherently selfish and in need of being taught how to cooperate with others, or are they inherently reliant on caregivers and in need of learning to be independent? These two different perspectives are probably both true in some sense, but one or the other can be stressed and help form the main parenting style in a home.

9.4 Frameworks

When we express a given perspective at a given time and place, it is almost always part of a much larger **framework** of connected claims and ideas than we can fully express at that time and place (Holland, Lachicotte, Jr.,

Skinner, & Cain 2001). We saw above that the scientist's professional journal article expresses perspectives that are part of the larger framework of coevolution theory in biology. The lower-socioeconomic white girl expresses a viewpoint on adults and authority that is also part and parcel of a larger framework of connected claims and ideas.

Frameworks can be formal theories in science or theory-like connected sets of claims and beliefs held by everyday people, often as part of their affiliation with different Discourses. Frameworks guide the perspectives we take in different situations and connect different, but related, perspectives we express across time. People are not necessarily consistent, because they can express contrary perspectives linked to two different frameworks tied to two different Discourses. Pro-life (anti-abortion) people believe (take the view, express the perspective) that abortion is murder because they have allegiance to a set of connected claims and beliefs about when life begins, the soul, religion, and the role of women in society, as well as other things. Pro-choice people believe that a woman has the right to choose because they have allegiance to a set of connected claims and beliefs about rights, bodies, the role of women, the limits of religion, and the nature of embryos, as well as other things.

We live today in a world where people with different frameworks, stemming from different families, educational backgrounds, communities, religions, cultures, institutions, and nations, not only disagree with each other, but often dismiss, denigrate, or even seek to harm others with different frameworks.

9.5 Reflective discussions

Every human has what we might call "cherished beliefs". These are beliefs that people are highly reluctant to give up. Thus, people are often not only reluctant to change them, but even to discuss them with other people who disagree with them, for fear they will lose their faith in what they cherish and need. In a highly polarized society we often try to stay with like-minded others in echo chambers defined by our shared cherished beliefs or we try, when we have to leave the echo chamber, to convert others, denigrate them, or even engage in violence.

So, we face a deep question: how can people in a diverse society engage in discussions about cherished beliefs—and other beliefs—in ways that unite and do not always divide? In a world like the one in which we live today, there is a pressing need for what I will call "reflective discussions".

Such discussions involve people respectfully discussing differing frameworks on important issues (Gutmann & Thompson 1996; Hess 2009).

The goal of such discussions is not to convert other people to "our side". It is not even to reach truth in the short run. The goal is that each party to such discussions will come—over time—to understand their own frameworks better, be able to argue for them at a conscious level, and may modify parts of them as they learn from others. The goal is also to appreciate the overall shape of other people's frameworks, not just as isolated claims, but in the contexts of their lived experiences. The ultimate goal is to test whether people, over time and with good will, can gradually converge, even if only partially, on frameworks that lead to a better world for all people, and, indeed, all living things (because all of us living beings are in this together).

What stands in the way of reflective discussions is the view, common on the right and left politically, that the goal of argument is to show someone else that they are wrong (or even stupid or evil). This does not work well to move people closer together and certainly not to recruit them to a common cause. Reflective discussions are based on thinking about truth not as a final destination, which we frail humans will not reach any time soon (or even ever), but as a journey where, over the long-haul, we may gradually converge on truth or, at least, a better form of life with each other.

Reflective discussions also crucially require that people respect the world in the sense that they seek to test parts of, or all of, their frameworks by acting in the world and paying respectful attention to what the world "says back" to their actions. The world that speaks back to us may be the natural world or the world of other people and social interactions.

Respectful attention to how the world "talks back" means two things: first, asking honestly whether the results the world gives back to our tests (actions followed by reflection) really support our beliefs and values, and, second, consulting with other people who differ from us in regard to how they assess the world's response to similar sorts of actions. This is just what "evidence" really means and it is basically the process that science formalizes. Again, the goal is not to prove someone—even yourself—right or wrong, once and for all, but for each of us to improve our frameworks in terms of the quality of our own lives and those of others with whom we share this planet.

If people do not respect the world's responses to their actions and beliefs, they cannot have a reflective discussion with others because they are not open to change. Equally, the responses of others to us in reflective discussions are also aspects of the world "talking back". These others, like us, were developed by society and the world in which we all live. One way or another, their frameworks are reflections of, and insights into, society and the world.

I am not saying that we should never criticize and never agitate against what we see as error or evil. But we can hardly understand other people's frameworks deeply enough to criticize them, if we have not respectfully listened to them and reflected fairly on their frameworks. Furthermore, none of us are in possession of anything like any final truth.

People who have enough goodwill to commit themselves to reflective discussions and to respecting the world and other people's responses to their actions are what I call "committed testers". And, remember, we are testing against the world as physical, social, cultural, and spiritual (in one of many senses people give this term). Such people realize that all frameworks and all cultures have flaws. As the Iranian philosopher Abdolkarim (Soroush 2000) has said "…each culture must disavow certain elements of itself". Soroush also captures well what it means to be a committed tester:

> We can have two visions of reason: reason as destination and reason as path. The first sees reason as the source and repository of truths. The second sees it as a critical, dynamic, yet forbearing force that meticulously seeks the truth by negotiating tortuous paths of trial and error. …
> (pp. 89–90).

Recommended reading

Abdolkarim A. Soroush (2000). *Reason, Freedom, and Democracy in Islam: Essential Writings of Abdolkarim Soroush*. Oxford: Oxford University Press.

9.6 Testing whole frameworks

Meaningful reflective discussions across different frameworks in science, religion, politics, or culture are not about vetting individual claims. They are about testing **whole frameworks** (all the claims in them as interrelated claims) against different ways of talking about and looking at experience.

In a reflective discussion we need to discuss and compare networks of claims that support each other, not a single claim out of the context of its supporting framework. We do not, for example, want to know whether someone thinks abortion is (or is not) murder. Rather, we want to get at the whole network of ideas, values, and knowledge claims in which this belief resides and from which it gets its meaning and support for a given person (Quine 1951).

Let me give a specific example of what I mean when I say that we do not test our frameworks claim by claim, but only in terms of the whole set or system of interrelated claims that compose the framework. For years now, one area in which I have worked is on the affordances of video games for good learning. I have made the claim that "good video games are good for learning" (in and out of school). But this claim is but one part of a set of claims that make up my framework (theory) about games and learning. Here is a simplified picture of my framework (Table 9.1) (Gee 2007):

When people do research to test my claim that video games are good for learning, they often have the view that science is about testing claims one by one to see if they are "true" or "a fact." But imagine that someone argued that they had shown my claim that video games are good for learning to be false based on evidence from their research. My claim is connected to a whole set of other claims. It does not rise or fall all by itself. Faced with their evidence I can change or adjust any one or more of these other claims and keep my claim that video games are good for learning. Perhaps I will say that the game they tested was not a "good game". Even if it was, I can modify my definition of "good game". I can adjust any of my claims or their relationships in my framework in a myriad of ways.

The point here is not that I can always "save" my claim from disconfirming evidence. Rather, the claim is I can speak to that evidence and make my framework better (empirically and otherwise) in a number of different ways. My point is also that you cannot really know what my claim means—what

TABLE 9.1 Video games are good for learning

Only good games are good for learning	Good = incorporate good learning principles	Learning = situated/ sociocultural approach
Good game = Good fit between game mechanics + interesting & challenging problems	Learning principles = from recent research in the learning sciences	Learning = mentored problem solving Learning = problem solving
Good game design is a form of teaching	Good = when integrated in a learning system, not stand alone	Learning requires teaching Teaching = well designed experiences Teaching = people, tools, design

the perspective on video games that claim expresses really amounts to—unless you work to discover my whole framework.

Any statement in my framework could have been bolded as the one people wanted to test or discuss, but things would still work the same. Any one statement brings all the others with it and the results of any test can be spoken to by a myriad of different adjustments. All we can ever do—in science, religion, politics, or culture—is honestly look at our frameworks and discuss them with others with different frameworks, draw logical consequences from the claims in our frameworks, and then seek to empirically respect the world and how it "talks back" to our actions and, in turn, ask ourselves how our own frameworks can be improved in the service of a better world, a better life, and the good of others.

If a pro-life person and a pro-choice person wanted to have a reflective discussion, they would have to become aware of the frameworks each of them operated within. It will not do—will not work—to simply debate the "facts" about when life begins in isolation (and, in fact, no empirical facts alone can determine the answer to this question). So, too, for a discussion between people about any other cherished beliefs. One central task of discourse analysis ought to be to uncover the frameworks that people have allegiance to, based on the various perspectives they take on an important issue across time in different contexts, and to help people come to understand and discuss in respectful and reflective ways their differing frameworks, even those that underwrite cherished beliefs.

Recommended reading

Karl R. Popper (1994). *The Myth of the Framework: In Defense of Science and Rationality*. London: Routledge.

9.7 Evidence, interpretation, and reflective discussions

I have argued that respect for evidence and engaging in respectful reflective discussions are crucial to what I have called becoming a "committed tester". However, it is important to understand the crucial role of **interpretation** in both reflecting on evidence and in engaging in critical discussions.

Any evidence we collect and any framework we have must be put into words if we are to reflect on them and discuss them with others; however, words do not have once-and-for-all fixed meanings. What a word means in context, as we have seen, varies across different contexts of use and it is not always easy to figure out what a word means in context. Often we have to work, reflect, and discuss with others in order to figure out what a given word means in a text or in talk. Sometimes, too, we have to negotiate with others what we are all going to mean by a word or we need to find new words to get past stumbling blocks.

One important context that we need to consider when we want to know the meanings of words is history. Consider, for instance, the Second Amendment to the US constitution and all the consternation it has caused in regard to guns. The Second Amendment says: "A well-regulated militia being necessary to the security of a free state, the right of the people to keep and bear arms shall not be infringed".

In his book, *The Second Amendment: A Biography*, Waldman (2014) points out that the world in which the Second Amendment was enacted would be unrecognizable to us today. In 1791, when the Bill of Rights was adopted, all white American males served in a state's militia for life. They purchased their own weapons, stored them in their homes, and brought them to battle when they needed to fight.

The Militia Acts, enacted in Congress in 1792, provided for the organization of state militias. At the time, there was no federal standing army. The Militia Acts authorized the president to take command of the state militias if invasion or insurrection was imminent. George Washington used this authority in 1794 to suppress the Whiskey Rebellion, a protest on the Western frontier against a new federal tax on whiskey (ironically, the Whiskey Rebels battle-cry was "No taxation without representation", something over which Washington had just fought a war with England).

Today, the militia is gone and the federal army is massive. Not every male is in the National Guard, let alone a militia. And soldiers do not supply their own weapons. So, does or does not the Second Amendment say that every American has the right to bear arms? How do we make sense of its "original" meaning now when its historical context is long gone? How can we construe its meaning for today and how close does this meaning have to be to its meaning in 1791?

We have a Supreme Court that makes decisions on issues like these, but their decision that the Second Amendment gives everyone the right to bear arms, including military-grade arms, has by no means ended controversy on the matter. For example, after he retired from the court, former Chief Justice Warren Burger—decrying the power of the gun lobby in the US AA—said that the Second Amendment "has been the subject of one of the greatest pieces of fraud—I repeat the word 'fraud'—on the American public by special interest groups that I have ever seen in my lifetime" (see: Biskupic 1995, p. A20).

Words, in our reflective discussions of frameworks with others, need to be interpreted. And that interpretation requires effort, education, and the realization that interpretation is a social—and, yes, historical and political—act. The study of language, culture, history, texts, and interpretation should be at the very heart of the education of any citizen in a society that wants to stay both civil and free.

9.8 Clashing frameworks in action

I want now to discuss an example of what happens when frameworks clash and there are no reflective discussions to mitigate this clash. Years ago, I worked in the town of Worcester, Massachusetts. Worcester, as we saw earlier, is a fascinating place. It has been a town since long before the USA became an independent country. For hundreds of years, Worcester has defined itself against Boston (the bigger, more prosperous, and prestigious city near it). In the colonial era, Worcester was "free soil" (opposed slavery and the return of escaped slaves), while Boston was much more tepid in these matters.

By the early 20th century, Worcester was a successful industrial working-class town. Its population was a mix of 19th-century "white" immigrants (from places like Poland, Russia, Ireland, and other parts of Europe) and African-Americans whose families went back to the Underground Railroad (the secret routes and waystations to freedom from slavery). This population "melted" (as in the "melting pot") into "Americans" primarily by becoming common citizens of Worcester first and foremost. Many teachers in Worcester's public schools had used teaching as a way to enter the middle class from working-class family backgrounds.

By the 1970s, Worcester's industrial base was beginning to decay, a victim of the out-sourcing of jobs. A once vibrant working-class community became financially depressed. Furthermore, the population of Worcester was fast "browning" due to a new wave of immigration from Asia, South America, Mexico, and the Caribbean. The teachers in the public schools, themselves a product of immigration, viewed the "brown" children in their classrooms as new "Worcester kids" and felt it was their job to help them become citizens of Worcester, and, thus, in that sense, to "melt" as had their own families.

Worcester has a number of good colleges and some years ago there was a project in one of them where university history professors and middle-school public school teachers worked together to design and teach a new history curriculum based on students engaging in local oral history. I was part of a team facilitating the meetings between the professors and teachers and also involved with studying their discourse practices.

The project went on for many meetings and eventually a curriculum was made and taught. However, the meetings were often contentious. From interviews, it became apparent that the professors thought the teachers were racists and the teachers thought the professors looked down on them and did not trust them. At one meeting a professor asked a teacher if she had much diversity in her classroom (which was, in fact, made up of white, Asian, South-American, Mexican, African-American, and Caribbean students). The teacher said, "No, they're all Worcester kids."

The professors wanted the middle-school kids to study their own neighborhoods (so, for example, a Vietnamese student would engage in oral history within a largely segregated Vietnamese neighborhood, which not so long ago had been, perhaps, a Polish neighborhood). The teachers wanted students to focus on the downtown of Worcester ("the center") and the people who went there from the socially and culturally diverse neighborhoods of Worcester.

The professors and the teachers never overtly discussed their conflicts or the possible sources of those conflicts. Eventually we noticed, however, that over the course of many meetings, the professors had used the words "diverse" and "diversity" many times, but never used words for having things "in common". The teachers, on the other hand, rarely used the word "diversity," but often used terms for having things in common as citizens of Worcester.

It became clear that the professors and the teachers brought two different frameworks to the meetings. Of course, people do not normally formalize their frameworks in explicit claims and so I cannot know the full details of their frameworks. However, as a discourse analyst, based on various sources of data, I can make hypotheses about their frameworks, given how the professors and teachers talked, interacted, acted, and expressed perspectives and values.

Here are simplified versions of the two different frameworks (Gee 2016): Professors:

1. Honoring diversity is the primary goal in schooling.
2. Diversity is defined in terms of race, class, and gender, but with a primary emphasis on race.

3. Stressing commonality over diversity is a form of colonization.
4. Failing to orient to a child's race or ethnicity is a form of racism.
5. Academics have privileged insight into the politics of race and diversity.
6. Larger macro-level power structures (the forces of states, politics, and institutions) systematically victimize "people of color," thereby severely limiting their agency at a local level.
7. Larger macro-level power structures are where the important causes and effects actually happen, though most people do not have the insight or knowledge to see this or really understand it.
8. Diverse neighborhoods should be the focus of Worcester, not the downtown, which is possibly unsafe anyway.
9. Teachers and the American public in general are not sophisticated intellectually or politically.
10. Teachers are locally focused; academics are nationally and globally focused.

Teachers:

1. Honoring commonality is the primary goal of Worcester public schooling.
2. The earlier "white" immigrants (their own families) and the even longer residing African-Americans "melted" into being co-citizens of Worcester and the new "brown" immigrants need to do so too.
3. One key goal of schooling is to make students become citizens of Worcester.
4. Placing children in large social groups effaces their individuality.
5. Teachers are there to teach individual children not "abstract" groups.
6. Class is more central than race or ethnicity in terms of people failing to get ahead.
7. The primary causes of people's success and failure are at the local level and a matter of their individual agency.
8. In a community where new immigrants are poor and often (the teachers believe) have dysfunctional families, teachers must not just teach, but nurture the children as individuals.
9. The downtown of Worcester needs to be a focus for everyone because that is where all the people of Worcester used to come together as citizens of Worcester. It needs to be revitalized.
10. Though college professors teach, they are not teachers.
11. Academics live in an Ivory Tower and do not know what is going on "on the ground".

Note that it will not do much good to pick one claim and ask whether it is true or pick one word and ask what it "really" means. This is so because each claim and each key word is inextricably linked to many of the other claims and words in each framework. It is not surprising that the professors felt the teachers were hiding things or even lying and the teachers felt the professors looked down on them and attributed racism to them.

In my own view, there are aspects of both frameworks that are wrong and aspects that are right. It will not do to pick one claim—for example, to dispute whether race or class is more important—in isolation. And, further, we need to explore what people mean by words like race and class, diversity and commonality, and teachers and teaching (e.g., Why are school teachers "teachers", but college professors are not?). In any case, a full honest civil reflective discussion of both frameworks as wholes could lead to deeper and better frameworks for both parties.

What might have happened if the participants in this project had seen the value of a reflective discussion comparing both frameworks in their entirety, with the goal not to convince each other about or settle in any final way a given claim or word meaning? The goal would have been for each party to come to a better understanding of their own framework, learn better ways to argue for it and explicate what it means, face new questions, and discover what parts of their framework, if any, they want to change or reformulate. Each party to such a discussion would respect evidence in the sense of how the world reacts to what they do and say when they use their framework in the world. In the end, they would all settle not for final truth or conversion, but for the possibility that transformed frameworks may gradually evolve and at least partially converge, in the course of critical discussions based on goodwill, towards frameworks that are truer, deeper, and more collaborative towards some common good.

9.9 Big "C" Conversations

Big D Discourses—socially recognizable ways of being different kinds of people—often existed before we were born and will go on existing long after we die. Discourses are partly defined in terms of their relationships of allegiance and opposition to each other. It is as if they use us humans (for our time on earth) to talk to, with, and against each other. Historically, Jews, Muslims, Catholics, and Protestants; capitalists, socialists, Marxists, and anarchists; different races, ethnic groups, nations, and cultures, and even the fans of competing sports teams, television shows, or video games, have defined themselves in relation to each other.

When we humans talk about the public debates that swirl around us in the media, in our reading, and in our interactions with other people, we are talking and taking part in debates among the Discourses that make up society. On certain large issues (e.g., abortion, smoking, gambling, feminism, affirmative action, etc.) nearly everyone in society knows what the "sides" are, how these sides are talked about and argued for, and what sort of people tend to be on specific sides. Some such issues are known by nearly everyone in a society, but others are known only by specifically defined groups (e.g., the ongoing big controversies in a given academic field). This knowledge about public issues and their sides is an ever-present background people bring to their interpretations of what they hear and read in media and society and to how they can formulate their own talk and writing.

I will call such public debates, arguments, motifs, issues, or themes "Conversations" with a capital "C", speaking metaphorically as if the various sides in debates around issues like abortion or smoking were engaged in one grand conversation (or debate or argument, whatever we want to call it). Of course, this big Conversation is composed of a myriad of interactional events taking place among specific people at specific times and places and within specific institutions.

Let me give you an example of what I am trying to get at here. It has for some time now been fashionable for businesses to announce (in "mission statements") their "core values" in an attempt to create a particular company "culture" (see Collins & Porras 1994, examples below are from pp. 68–69). For instance, at one time, the announced core values of Johnson & Johnson, a large pharmaceutical company, included "The company exists to alleviate pain and disease" and "Individual opportunity and reward based on merit", as well as several others.

One might wonder, then, what the core values of a cigarette company might be. Given the Conversations that most Americans are familiar with— about the USA and its history, as well as about smoking—we can almost predict what they will be. For example, the espoused core values of Philip Morris, a large company that sells cigarettes among a great many other products, once included "The right to personal freedom of choice (to smoke, to buy whatever one wants) is worth defending", "Winning—being the best and beating others", and "Encouraging individual initiative", as well as (in a statement similar to one of Johnson & Johnson's statements) "Opportunity to achieve based on merit, not gender, race, or class."

We all readily connect Philip Morris's core value statements to themes of American individualism and freedom. We can interpret these statements in light of what we know about various Conversations that have gone on historically in the USA not just over smoking itself, but also over freedom, individuality, government, and other topics. Conversations interact and affect each other. Note how the values of "individual initiative" and "reward for merit", which are part of the core values of both Johnson & Johnson and Philip Morris, take on a different coloring in the two cases. In the first case, they take on a humanistic coloring and in the other the coloring of "every man for himself". This coloring is the effect of our knowledge of the two sides to the "smoking Conversation" in which, we all know, individual freedom is pitted against social responsibility. This debate has gone on now for decades and is, perhaps, near its end in places like the USA where social responsibility, coupled with heath issues and healthcare costs, are close to winning out and closing the historical debate over smoking in favor of not doing it.

Note here, then, how values, beliefs, and objects play a role in the sorts of Conversations I am talking about. We know that in this Conversation some people will hold values and beliefs consistent with expressions about individualism, freedom, the "American way", and so forth, while others will express values and beliefs consistent with the rights of others, social responsibility, and protecting people from harm, even harm caused by their own desires. In turn, these two values and belief orientations can be historically tied to much wider dichotomies centering around beliefs about the responsibilities and the role of governments.

Furthermore, within this Conversation, an object like a cigarette or an institution like a tobacco company, or an act like the act of smoking itself, take on meanings—symbolic values—within the Conversation, but dichotomous meanings. Smoking can be seen as an addiction, an expression of freedom, or a lack of caring about others. The point is that those familiar with the Smoking Conversation, and the other Conversations it engages with, know the possible meanings of cigarettes, tobacco companies, and smoking.

The themes and values that enter into Conversations circulate in a multitude of texts and media. They are the products of historical disputes between and among different Discourses. Think, for example, of the historical debate between the Discourse of evolutionary biologists and the Discourse of fundamentalist creationists. This debate, over time, has constituted a Conversation that many people in society know something about. For that reason it is hard for a newspaper to discuss evolution in any terms without triggering people to think about this debate and to try to interpret what the newspaper is saying in terms of it.

People are often unaware of specific historical clashes among Discourses (e.g., the Reformation, the history of creationism, the changing nature of feminist Discourses). Often they are only aware of the residue of issue, debates, claims, and clashes that make up Big C Conversations. Historical interactions of Discourses leads to certain debates ("Conversations") (for example, debates over smoking, race, evolution, global warming, and the "nature" of men and women, and gays), being known widely by people in a society or social group, even by people who are not themselves members of those Discourses or even aware of their histories.

Recommended reading

Michael Billig (1987). *Arguing and Thinking: A Rhetorical Approach to Social Psychology*. Cambridge: Cambridge University Press.

9.10 The end

We have reached the end of our journey. It has been a journey from grammar to discourse to society. It has also been a journey from choices to perspectives to frameworks and, we hope, to a better world. There are, as I said at the outset, many different approaches to discourse analysis. I have flown you high above the forest. You must choose where to land and settle. But all approaches to discourse must lead to better mutual understanding for a better world or they are not worth doing in this troubled, imperiled world we all share.

References

Biskupic, J. (1995). Guns: A Second (Amendment) Look. *Washington Post*, Wednesday, May 10, p. A20.

Collins, J. C. & Porras, J. I. (1994). *Built to Last: Successful Habits of Visionary Companies*. New York: Harper Business.

Gee, J. P. (2007). *What Video Games Have to Teach Us About Learning and Literacy*. Second Edition. New York: Palgrave/Macmillan.

Gee, J. P. (2016). Discourse Matters: Bridging Frameworks. *Journal of Multicultural Discourses* 11.4: 343–349.

Gutmann, A. & Thompson, D. (1996). *Democracy and Disagreement*. Cambridge, MA: Belknap Press.

Harkness, S., Super, C. M., & Keefer, C. H. (1992). Learning to Be an American Parent: How Cultural Models Gain Directive Force. In R. D'Andrade & C. Strauss, Eds, *Human Motives and Cultural Models*. Cambridge: Cambridge University Press, pp. 163–178.

Hess, D. (2009). *Controversy in the Classroom. The Democratic Power of Discussions*. New York: Routledge.

Holland, D., Lachicotte, Jr., W. S., Skinner, D., & Cain, C. (2001). *Identity and Agency in Cultural Worlds*. Cambridge, MA: Harvard University Press.

Lewontin, R. C. (1991). *Biology as Ideology: The Doctrine of DNA*. New York: Harper.

MacWhinney, B. (2000). Perspective-Taking and Grammar. *Japanese Society for the Language Sciences* 1.1: 1–25.

MacWhinney, B. (2005). The Emergence of Grammar from Perspective. In D. Pecher & R. A. Zwaan, Eds, *Grounding Cognition: The Role of Perception and Action in Memory, Language, and Thinking*. Mahwah, NJ: Lawrence Erlbaum, pp. 198–223.

Mercer, H. & Sperber, D. (2017). *The Enigma of Reason*. Cambridge, MA: Harvard University Press.

Myers, G. (1990). *Writing Biology: Texts in the Social Construction of Scientific Knowledge*. Madison, WI: University of Wisconsin Press.

Quine, W. V. O. (1951). Two Dogmas of Empiricism. *The Philosophical Review* 60.1: 20–43.

Rommetveit, R. (1974). *On Message Structure: A Framework for the Study of Language and Communication*. New York: Wiley.

Rommetveit, R. (1980). On "Meanings" of Acts and What Is Meant by What Is Said in a Pluralistic Social World. In M. Brenner, Ed., *The Structure of Action*. Oxford: Blackwell and Mott, pp. 108–149.

Schegloff, E. A. (1997). Whose Text? Whose Context? *Discourse & Society* 8.2: 165–187.

Silverstein, M. (1992). The Indeterminacy of Contextualization: When Is Enough Enough? In P. Auer & A. Di Luzio, Eds, *The Contextualization of Language*. Amsterdam: John Benjamins, pp. 55–76.

Soroush, A. A. (2000). *Reason, Freedom, and Democracy in Islam: Essential Writings of Abdolkarim Soroush*. Oxford: Oxford University Press.

Sperber, D. & Wilson, D. (1986). *Relevance: Communication and Cognition*. Cambridge, MA: Harvard University Press.

Sperber, D. & Wilson, D. (1996). Fodor's Frame Problem and Relevance Theory. *Behavioral and Brain Sciences* 19.3: 530–532.

Tracy, K. (2010). Analyzing Context: Framing the Discussion. *Research on Language and Social Interaction* 31.1: 1–28.

van Dijk, T. A. (2008). *Discourse and Context: A Sociocognitive Approach*. Cambridge: Cambridge University Press.

Waldman, M. (2014). *The Second Amendment: A Biography*. New York: Simon & Schuster.

Index